You're not the boss of me

You're not the boss of me

Adventures of a Modern Mom

ERIKA SCHICKEL

KENSINGTON BOOKS
http://www.kensingtonbooks.com

KENSINGTON BOOKS are published by

Kensington Publishing Corp.
850 Third Avenue
New York, NY 10022

All Kensington titles, imprints and distributed lines are available at special quantity discounts for bulk purchases for sales promotion, premiums, fundraising, educational or institutional use.

Special book excepts or customized printings can also be created to fit specific needs. For details, write or phone the office of the Kensington Special Sales Manager: Kensington Publishing Corp., 850 Thirde Avenue, New York, NY 10022. Attn. Special Sales Department. Phone: 1-800-221-2647.

Kensington and the K logo Reg. U.S. Pat. & TM Off.

ISBN 0-7582-1537-1

First Kensington Trade Paperback Printing: January 2007
10 9 8 7 6 5 4 3 2 1

Printed in the United States of America

To Franny and Georgia:
The subjects of my story,
the objects of my love

Acknowledgments

As with children, books are rarely birthed by one lone, frightened woman. I had many midwives on this, without whom I would still be pregnant with a zygote of an idea and heading into my twentieth trimester.

My father, Richard Schickel, told me during this process that "publishing is like dying, you do it alone," and then he disproved it by giving me his unstinting creative and professional support. That, along with his daily, lifelong example that writer's block is for sissies, got me to the finish line. I also owe so much to my mother, Julia Whedon, whose eloquence in all things taught me that language, whether written, spoken or spelled out on a Boggle board, is a sandbox to be played in. My sister, Jessica Schickel, who will always be the writer I aspire to be, gave me an early and generous reading that helped steer me.

Thanks to David L. Ulin, my dear friend and mentor, who, by example and encouragement, turned me from a private scribbler into a professional (and somewhat mercenary) writer. Deepest heartfelt thanks also to my best friend and partner in many a mommy misdemeanor, Rae Dubow. Rae, my books will always be in the locker.

I am so beholden to Nicole Diamond Austin, my first agent at The Creative Culture who found me on the Internet, tracked me down, and convinced me to write this book. Also to her successor, Laura Nolan, whose steady, patient professionalism has been the scaffolding holding this whole rig up. Thanks also to Kensington Books and Audrey LaFehr for popping my book publishing cherry.

Several of these pieces originally appeared in other venues. Thanks to Hip Mama, Rhino Records, the *LA Weekly,* and *Los Angeles City Beat.* Also, a long-overdue thanks to Susan Lowenberg at LA Theatre Works, who produced my kooky one-woman show *Wild Amerika* ten years ago which was the seed pod of this book.

Deep gratitude goes to my writing group, who stood by with hot towels and told me to push. Dinah Lenney, Sariah Dorbin and Marjorie Sa'adah, Mark Katz, Vanina Marsot, and Brenda Freiberg. These generous readers and gifted writers always made me feel like my stuff, no matter how rough, was the highlight of their day. I am likewise indebted to the other extraordinarily gifted writers who have given me their esteemed friendship and support: Robert Lloyd, Judith Lewis, and Barbara Isenberg.

I owe so much to my good buddy Mark Netter. Sometimes we meet people who sign up for us whole-heartedly and for life, and though we're never quite sure why we're so lucky, we're eternally grateful. Mark is such a friend, giving me encouragement, feedback, and inspiration for nearly twenty years.

I must also thank my friend Tamara Mugalian without whose kinship, humor, and expertise I might not have made it through the first two years of motherhood. Tamara, you are my model of what a truly good mother is, and I will be forever grateful for you and your family's influence over me and my family.

Thanks to the parents and teachers at Canfield Avenue Elementary, who are the extraordinary village I have relied on to help me raise my children—and get some work done. I never dreamed going back to grade school would teach me so much.

Thanks to Bennett, who restored my faith in felines and taught me to love again. And, of course, thanks to Mike Durgan.

My biggest debt of gratitude is to my beloved husband, Doug Freeman. Co-parent, partner, sweetheart, proofreader, balance-tipper, and all-around handyman, my life would be utterly broken without him. Doug has also done dogged service as my own, private Strunk and White, vetting every word I have ever written including these. (Sweets, why should I learn the rule about semicolons when I have you?)

Lastly, and most importantly, thanks to my darling daughters Frances Grace and Georgia Mae Freeman. Every day with you is a present I get to open. I hope you don't read this book until you're *much* older, but when you do, I hope you'll understand.

Contents

The Obstetrical Dilemma

"I am fearfully and wonderfully made."—Psalms 139:14

Unsafe sex is so hot. After years of pills and latex, foams and jellies, Doug and I took it all off. Skin on skin, every cell firing in perfect, natural unencumbrance. Unprotected sex is a whole reason for getting knocked up. We made our firstborn child doggie style. As I hump my beloved, in the back of my head I think, *this can't possibly work—it's just too much fun.*

After four glorious years of celebrating our love and our marriage, the perfect union of our souls, my husband, Doug, and I begin feeling like the whole thing is getting old. Not the relationship, necessarily, but just our endless absorption in ourselves and each other. We want to widen our focus and we think a baby might be just the ticket.

Two days later I buy a home pregnancy test and pee on the stick. A blue line appears. *Holy crap, it worked!*

I immediately call my friend Tamara, who has birthed two children in a bathtub, which, in my book, qualifies her for midwifery. The phone is answered and I can hear a toddler's heavy breathing on the other end, but no greeting of any kind.

"Hello? Olivia? Is your mommy there? Let me talk to her." The phone drops with a clatter. A long silence ensues in which I go mad thinking the girl has forgotten to tell her mom. Then Tamara's exhausted voice comes on: "Hello?"

"Hey, Tamara, it's me."

"Oh—hey, Erika, hold on a second . . . Emory, take Olivia's Beanie Baby out of the toilet and give it back to her *this minute*. Sorry, Erika—what's up?"

"Oh, nothing, really, except I took a home pregnancy test this morning and it came out positive."

Tamara, who is solidly pro-procreation, who had children before any of her friends and was longing for some company in the trenches, whoops into the phone, "All *right!*"

"You don't actually think that means I'm pregnant, do you?"

"Um . . . *yeah.*"

A zygote of fear forms in the pit of my stomach. Oh dear Lord, what have I done? Everything was *fine* the way it was. Life was good with just me and Doug. We don't need some kid horning in and tying us down. And what about my career? I mean, I had just gotten two lines on *Murphy Brown,* I was finally making it as an actress, and now I am sabotaging myself with a fucking *baby?* Why would I want to go and mess with things when I am already so totally perfect?

An image haunted me. It could best be described as a Hallmark Moment: A soft-focus, pregnant woman in a gauzy nightie stands in front of a sunlit window. Her huge, swollen abdomen is seen in silhouette through the sheer scrim of fabric. She lovingly caresses her belly with a secret smile on her lips.

It seems to me that pregnancy belongs to a kind of woman beyond my ken. Kind, soft, contented Breck girls. Considerate, responsible gentlewomen who own and wear matching bra-and-panty sets and can discuss douching with straight faces. Not women like me—cussing, nail-biting, ego-driven women who at the age of thirty-two still think Lucky Charms are magically delicious.

I look down at the Clearblue Easy stick in my lap. Just a scrap of litmus paper stuck to a plastic Popsicle stick. I think—*hold on a minute*... I am allowing my life to be completely turned around by what some piece-of-shit, ten-dollar home pregnancy test says? So I do what any reasonable woman in my situation would do: I go out and buy a *twelve-dollar* home pregnancy test. This time there is no blue line. There is a pink plus sign.

Not being one for midwives and hot tubs myself, I find an obstetrician named Beazy. Beyond her spotless medical qualifications, I like her for her lighthearted, can-do approach toward obstetrics. I also like the fact that in addition to the hundreds of children she has brought into the world—three were through her very own vagina.

"So, Erika, what day did your last period start on?" Normally, this is a trick question for me. I am not one of those women who circles dates in red pen or looks to the moon to keep track of her cycle. But it happened that my last period arrived on New Year's Day, making it memorable, even to me.

"Okay, let's take a look here..." Beazy pulled a little laminated wheel out of her white coat pocket, and in an odd moment of destiny roulette, spins the dial. *Round and round she goes, where she stops, nobody knows.* My due date comes up October 8. We schedule an appointment for a full examination, and I grab my purse and my husband, thinking it's time to go. Beazy says . . . "Wait, don't you want to hear the baby's heartbeat?"

"Can we?" It hardly seems possible.

We go into an exam room and she has me pull up my shirt and undo my pants button. She places a little mic attached to a tiny speaker on my still-flat abdomen, and there it is . . . the little muffled tom-tom that is my baby's heart. Fast and strong and liquid, it beats with such ferocity! It is doing double-time to my own, slow thud a mere eight inches to the north. Two hearts, both mine. The timpani of my life.

The first trimester is mostly a state of mind. The secret I carry is way bigger than the embryo itself. It's a secret I can't keep. I tell everybody. Friends, family, Ken the water delivery guy. Everybody is overjoyed and treats me as though I were as precious as a Fabergé egg.

Soon I hunger for more information about the baby. Needing a visual aid, I go to the bookstore for something that will show me the baby's development in *pictures*. Amid the rows and rows of baby books, I find one volume that seemed to fit the bill: *Your Pregnancy Week-by-Week*. I draw out the book and look at its cover and gasp, for there she is: the hugely pregnant Stepford Mommy—gauzy nightie and all, feeling all the beautiful wonderment of her womanhood. It is my Hallmark nightmare fully realized. *No, I can't do it. It's too horrible.* I can't bear the thought of having this book on my bedside table. I search desperately for another book that would suit, but no, everything else is just parenting advice. I bring Mrs. Stepford Mommy home with me to be my tour guide through pregnancy.

Week 1—The embryo is the size of the head of a pin.

A pinhead. A polka dot of a person. A mere smidge of something which is really, to me, only theoretical. These are my thoughts as I grab a shopping cart and push it through the automatic doors of the grocery store. Beazy had given me a copy *of What to Expect When You're Expecting* and the *Best Odds Diet* looms like a dare. Could I do it, I wondered? Could I give up my evil ways and start eating healthy foods at every meal? It would be a mighty sacrifice, and all in the interests of this theoretical being housed next door to my stomach. I steer my cart past an I.M.Pei-sized pyramid of Coca-Cola, over to the produce aisle. I load up my cart with healthy fruits and vegetables, vowing to turn over a new lettuce leaf. Feeling resolve, I reach for the kale, a vegetable that has always scared me. Suddenly, I am assaulted by the most nauseating smell I have ever known. I look behind me to the source of the stench: a 4'x4' crate of onions. The pungent odor smells like overripe tube socks lightly sautéed in Crisco. It rolls up through my stomach and bile rises in my throat. I drop the kale and head for the nearest exit. Dry-heaving out in the parking lot, I decide this baby is just going to have to make do with what it gets. I may never eat again.

Week 4—The embryo is half the size of a typewritten "O."

I grow boobs! Big, beautiful B-cups! My first-ever, bona-fide rack. I spend hours in front of the mirror playing with them, admiring them, trying different outfits on them. I go bra shopping and buy them underwires and demi-cups and extra hooks. All the styles I could never find in an A-cup. I lift and separate them. I push them together and stare into my plunging cleavage. I work those puppies like a Vegas showgirl. Big boobs are the ultimate accessory. Who knew?

Week 12—*The fetus is now the size of a fist.*

By the end of the first trimester I am still not showing, but my pants are kind of tight. I rush out and purchase my first maternity item: a large pair of overalls. I excitedly climb into them, not realizing that I am going to spend the next *two years* of my life in them.

Week 15—*The fetus is the size of a softball.*

Late one night, during Letterman, I feel a flutter. Like a tiny moth is inside of me, beating its wings. That's when I start to believe.

Week 18—*The baby is now the size of an open hand.*

I dream that I have given birth to triplets. I check out of the hospital and pile the swaddled babies into the back of a Checker cab and take them home without looking at them. When I get home I put them in their playpen and fall into bed, exhausted from childbirth. I sleep for hours and hours. Finally I am awakened by the pitiful wails of my hungry babies. I get up and go to the playpen to look at my children for the first time and . . . ! What I find are three jaundiced, wiry little boys—no, not boys, tiny, little man-babies. They appear to be Armenian and all have miniature five o'clock shadows. There must have been some mix-up at the hospital! They simply can't be mine. But it's too late—I am stuck with them and must figure out a way to love them. The boys are hungry and growling for milk. I put their scratchy, toothy little faces to my breasts and nurse them.

Week 20—Your baby is now the size of a small clutch purse.

One morning, as I am changing out of my gauzy nightie and into my overalls, Doug looks at me and says, "Honey, you've popped!"

Sure enough, I had become visibly pregnant overnight. I feel profound relief. Now the whole world could see that I am not a fat cow, I am a *pregnant* cow.

The first outsider to notice my delicate condition is Jeff, the sofa salesman at Plummer's. He suggests getting our new sofa Soil Shielded. "Since you're having a baby," he explains. "They can be really messy, you know."

"You mean you can tell I'm pregnant?"

"Oh, sure. What are you, five months gone?"

Suddenly, I feel a rush of affection for this perky little sofa salesman and I happily plunk down the extra seventy-five bucks. After all, I will be a mother, and Soil Shielding is the kind of protective, responsible thing mothers do.

Week 25—Your baby is now the size of a crock pot.

I am undeniably pregnant. Everybody sees it and everybody wants to talk about it.

"It's a boy—you're carrying high."

"It's a girl—you're carrying it behind you."

The armchair obstetricians are everywhere. The Starbucks clerk looks up from foaming my latte and says, "Hey man, should you be drinking coffee?"

The Lenscrafters optician asks me how much weight I have gained so far. The Blockbuster clerk wants to know if I plan to deliver vaginally.

Week 30—Your baby is now the size of a Butterball turkey.

As a pregnant woman, I have become public property. Strangers come up to me on the street and lay their hands on my belly. Without asking. Like I'm a Buddha or the Blarney Stone, or I'm wood to knock on and I will bring them luck. All I give them in return is the hairy eyeball. I want to tell them to fuck off and mind their own goddamn business, but that kind of surly attitude would make me a spoilsport and clearly unfit to bear children.

Week 33—Your baby is now the size of a bus wheel.

I have moved out of the quaintly pregnant stage, and into the realm of the startling. I am gaining weight exponentially. The baby has pushed my stomach up under my ribs and I suffer from chronic heartburn. Every night I chew a couple of Tums and bed down with a complex scaffolding of pillows to support various parts of my now grotesque anatomy.

I suffer from a chronic skin rash known quaintly as PUPPP, or pruritic urticarial papules and plaques of pregnancy. It breaks out up and down my legs and packs a bitch of an itch. But the greatest indignity of all . . . my feet and ankles have become so swollen I have resorted to wearing . . . *Birkenstocks.*

It is August and in the 90s every day. When I sit down,

the undersides of my breasts become glued to the top of my belly.

Week 36—Your baby is now the size of a Barcalounger.

I am body-snatched. This person has become a bad tenant. It feels like someone has moved into me and rearranged all the furniture. I am bumping into myself—and yet it is not myself anymore. It is this person I am supposed to love unconditionally. Well, pardon my skepticism, but this person isn't exactly *endearing* his- or herself to me. I lie in bed at night, acid roiling up from my cramped stomach like a red-hot comet, and think, *I won't be able to love the baby. What if it's a dud? What if I'm a dud? What if it's too big to come out?*

Until now, I wasn't nervous about the actual birth. You see, I've lived a lucky life and I've never really known physical pain. But looking at my now-humungous belly, I'm thinking I'm gonna find out. I'm wishing Doug and I hadn't goofed off so much in Lamaze class. How do I possibly prepare for this event? My articulate, straightforward girlfriends who have birthed are all aggravatingly vague. They can't remember it well enough to describe it. They all say, "It's worth it." Worth what? Hideous suffering? Astonishing pain?

Week 39—Your baby is now the size of Marlon Brando.

I want it out! I go see Beazy on the sixth of October, the day the O.J. verdict is to be announced. I have made a secret bet with myself: if O.J. is found guilty it would mean I'm having the baby on my due date. If he's found not guilty, then I will indeed be pregnant for the rest of my life.

Sitting on the exam table, my belly straining the seams on my paper dress, I hear some hubbub out in the waiting room. Beazy comes in and informs me the verdict has been rendered: The Juice is a free man. We are both silent for a stunned moment. She cannot believe the injustice of such evil going unpunished, while I cannot believe the injustice of O.J. being free to golf and go about his nefarious business while I have been sentenced to life in this flesh prison.

October 7 comes and goes, and childbirth now seems like a mythical event I will never get to experience. It's clear that pregnancy is just a giant pro-life conspiracy to get women on their backs and keep them there. I become enraged.

October 8, my due date, and this kid is still on the wrong side of my belly button. I take long walks, I scarf tons of balsamic vinaigrette, I screw Doug morning, noon, and night in a vain attempt to induce labor. *Still pregnant.* I try jumping up and down. I have more sex. I sob into my pillow. Doug guiltily pats me on the head. Of course, he realizes this is all his fault and he must suffer, too.

The morning of October 9, I haul my Jabba-the-Hut-like body out of bed and feel a warm, wet trickle down my leg. It's clear and sweet-smelling. *Amniotic fluid. My water broke! That's it*? I had always imagined a dramatic splash, a puddle, mopping up.

We go to the hospital and a sonogram confirms what over the last few months I have come to fear: *I am having a big-ass baby.* Beazy pulls up a chair and gives me my options: "Now Erika, this baby is well over ten pounds. By law I have to offer you a C-section. But I think if anyone can deliver this baby vaginally . . . you can."

I don't know whether to be heartened or offended by this comment. I wonder, *Can anyone deliver this baby? Anyone other than me? Because, vaginally speaking, I don't think I'm up to the task.*

By three o'clock in the afternoon, labor hasn't begun. The baby doesn't want to come down to the front desk and check out of Hotel Moi. So it's time to evict. Beazy gives the order to start the Pitocin and induce labor.

Which brings us to what is known anthropologically as "The Obstetrical Dilemma." I had often wondered why giving birth is so easy for four-legged animals. Horses? Dogs? Cows? *Elephants?* Those are some big babies and the mama just pants a little, squeezes out her litter, licks them off, whips out a tit, and takes a nap.

But for us humans . . . damn, it hurts. I mean . . . *wow.* It starts out slow and the pain just gets on a roll and there's no way out of it. No way. No way. Nothing helps, not rubbing it, squeezing a hand, blowing on it, ice, heat, up, down . . . No, OH! Oh, and then it fades for a minute, it . . . goes . . . away . . . and you can breathe for a moment and you love that moment, you want it to stay, you want to roll it around on your tongue and suck every last second out of it. But you know it won't last much longer, and that makes you not able to truly enjoy this blissfully pain-free passage because the big Santa belt they have strapped around your belly is picking up the baby's heartbeat, which is getting faster for the next contract-oh, ho, ho, ho, it's PARTY TIME AGAIN and OH MY FUCKING GOD, Ican'tdothisIcan'tithurtstoomuchtodotodoIwanttogohomepleasegetmeoutofhere NOWWWWWOWWWOWWWW!!!!

Two events occurred in the course of human evolution which caused what is known to anthropologists as The Obstetrical Dilemma: first, we learned to walk upright. Bipedalism led to a smaller, fused pelvis, to bear and balance all that vertical weight.

So, in fact, childbirth was easier for us millions of years ago, *when we still walked on our knuckles.* Now, I'm essentially *for* bipedalism. It did, after all, lead to the invention of shoes, which I *love*. But why should women pay the whole evolutionary price? It's not *fair*. I want men to suffer, too! I want a refund! I want free shoes!!! ... I want ... I want ... I want ... I want ... DRUGS!!!!

I've never said no to drugs before, so why start now? And here's a little secret: *Lamaze doesn't work*. I get my epidural and in a single magic moment I am pain-free and able to think clearly again.

Which brings me to the second evolutionary hitch in The Obstetrical Dilemma: big brains. As we humans got smarter, our brains got bigger and so did our skulls. Now, not only are women saddled with fused pelvises, but we're having to squeeze extra-big-headed babies through our girdles! Again, there is a price for everything, but again, I feel that the cost burden is placed entirely, and unfairly, on the female. To think that men should then have the hubris to deny women the right to choose whether or not to go through this agony makes my own big head spin. It makes me hate them so *much*! Especially the one I am married to, who is standing at my feet right now, telling me to "Push, honey, push!"

Once, when I was a little girl, I asked my mother what it felt like to give birth. She said, "Honey, it feels like you are having the world's biggest b.m." She was right. It's the same sense of urgency. I'm conscious of little else. My brain has shut down like an office building at night—only a few floors are lit up. Every ounce of wattage I have is focused on getting this frigging thing out of my body.

I train my focus on a spot on the wall above Beazy's head. A decorative seascape photo hangs there, but I can only describe the one seagull that flies in its amber-hued sky. The bird's wings are extended, making it a perfect X. I stare at that white X and push as hard as I can. I take every scrap of focus I have left after fourteen hours of labor, and I project it all onto the back of that seagull. Each contraction is a fresh opportunity to pummel Jonathan Livingston Fuckbird with intention, with will, with the animal need to purge.

Somehow, in the process of giving birth, I completely forgot about the baby. So when something warm and heavy is placed on my belly, I am confused. What the hell is this? A wet towel?

I look up for the first time in hours for an explanation. There is Doug! He has put on hospital scrubs at some point. His face is drawn and haggard. His hair is greasy and on crooked. He has grown a beard. He is weeping and smiling as he leans in and in a choked voice he says, "Honey, honey, it's a girl!"

I look down at the shining, pink creature curled up on my belly. I put my hands on her hot, slippery body and gather her up to me. She is covered in gunk that smells green and pure, like mulch. It is fresh life I am smelling. We are both wailing and sobbing with the shock and joy of seeing each other. I am shaking like a leaf, not with cold, just rattling uncontrollably as I put her to my breast. She takes it immediately, her tiny mouth pulling fiercely on my startled nipple. The room grows quiet as we all watch in awe this amazing display of instinct. *Of course* I can love this baby. This perfectly evolved human being. This ten-pound, seven-ounce daughter, Frances Grace Freeman.

Pussy Belly

The dressing room at Loehmann's is one of the toughest in Los Angeles. It is a big, communal room. Long benches line the mirrored walls, which are punctuated with hooks. Women of all shapes and sizes crowd into it, staking out a hook and a couple of feet of bench. Then they strip down to varying states of seminudity. The harsh lighting and facing mirrors reflect one's dimpled flesh into infinity, and usually results, for me, in a crisis of confidence.

Just my luck—the only vacant span of mirror is next to a lovely, twenty-ish girl with the build of a sandpiper. I park four-and-a-half-year-old Franny on the bench and hang up my two dresses to try on. The girl next to me is wiggling out of her halter top and jeans. She is wearing a G-string and has nothing to hide. I, on the other hand, keep my eyes off the mirror as I undress. I get into the first dress, a tasteful, sand-colored linen frock. Comfortable and sensible. I look to Franny, who is engrossed in a bouquet of hang tags she has scavenged off the floor.

"What do you think, honey?"

Franny casts a quick and steady eye over me and says, "That dress makes me feel like to throw up, Mommy."

The sandpiper girl, overhearing this, cannot suppress a laugh. We exchange a look.

"Well, then I guess I won't get this one," I reply, taking the dress off and putting it back on the hanger. I pick up the other dress, a stretchy, short, crocheted number. Very Missoni-meets-Hervé Leger, its multicolors running in raucous, horizontal waves. This is the kind of dress that would look good with leather boots and long hair, neither of which I happen to have. It's a clingy dress, and so my hopes are necessarily low as I shimmy into it. When I turn to the mirror I am amazed. The psychedelic pattern has worked some kind of optical illusion. I am magically transformed from a tired, slouchy mom . . . into a hippity-hip-hopping-groovalicious, trollopsizing Fly Grrrl.

Franny looks at me with a wide grin; "You look like candy, Mama." The sandpiper girl nods in agreement. For a mere $29.99, I am candy.

Two days later, I am standing at the sink when I hear the afternoon mail fall through the slot with a smack. I shuffle over and paw through the supermarket circulars and assorted Pottery Barn catalogues in search of some actual first-class mail. One piece. My Cinderella heart skips a beat. My invitation to The Medicine Ball has arrived.

In a town where parties are thrown like confetti, only one crumb falls to me each year: the Sweet Relief Medicine Ball, which benefits sick and uninsured musicians.

I withdraw the heavy card and it accordions open to look like an old-time circus poster. In Gothic letters is the name of the headliner: Patti Smith. My heart goes into a trot and a little squeal of excitement bursts out of me, sounding like, "Yeeeeee!"

Patti Smith was my heroine in high school. She spoke to

my teenage rebel heart. She was tortured, poetic, and iconoclastic, *just like me.* Most importantly, *Patti rocked.* And now, nearly twenty years later, I would finally get to see her live. I suddenly remember the magic dress hanging in my closet and my entire cosmic axis just seems to slide into place.

I sashay over to my closet to try on the dress and work my sweet, sassy stuff for a minute in the privacy of my bedroom. I might even try some shoes and a couple of, *Hey, Patti's.* I open the door and there it is, vibing on its plastic hanger. I wriggle into the slinky tube and turn to the mirror ready to see the Candy Girl.

But something terrible and inexplicable has happened. The magic has disappeared from the dress. It's become an optical nightmare. The psychadelic wave pattern has become *horizontal stripes.* I don't look hip, but hippy. Like a hip-hippity-hippo. In two short days I had gone from fabulous to flabulous. But why? How?

Is it possible that I was wrong about Loehmann's dressing room? Could it have been the dressing room that was magic? Some alchemical interplay of fluorescence and infinity mirrors? When I look straight into my very own mirror, my thighs look like a pair of Easter hams packed into a tiny string bag. I turn my back to the mirror and look over my shoulder to get the rear view. My ass, in this dress, looks like a loudly upholstered bolster cushion. Then I execute a quarter turn and am confronted by the most horrifying sight of all: Pussy Belly.

Horror rises in my throat and escapes my lips with a sound like, "Aaaaaaaiiiaaaiiiiaaaii!!" A sound that Patti Smith herself might make were she to write a song about Pussy Belly, which, of course, she would never ever have to do.

* * *

"Pussy Belly" is a term coined by a boyfriend I had in my early twenties. It denotes the little prolapse of fat located on women between the navel and the pubis. He would point out women in public with extreme cases of "P.B.," enlisting me in his mockery of them. I would scoff at these poor hags, too. What did I know? I was twenty-three years old and had a girl's long, lean belly. I could not fathom then how these sorry old dames had let themselves go.

But now, two babies and fifteen years later, my very own Pussy Belly hangs, like a fanny pack in reverse, in glorious reprimand for all my youthful disdain.

I try to suck it in, but Pussy Belly cannot be sucked in. Even as all the surrounding stomach muscles tighten, she hangs all the jigglier. Pussy Belly will not be easily beaten. I need Lycra, and lots of it.

I call my friend Rae, literally, for support.

"I just tried on the party dress."

"The Missoni?"

"Yes. Oh God, I think I need a girdle."

"Oh, I'm so sorry." Rae is a very understanding and sensible person. "Go to Miss Stevens's."

"Who?"

"The lingerie store near Doheny. Kathy got her Emmy girdle there. They really know fit." She delivers this statement in her most confident, I-am-a-Jewish-woman-who-knows-of-what-she-speaks tone of voice. It gives me strength.

"Okay, I'll go. But I'm scared."

I expect a tiny hole-in-the-wall shop stacked floor to ceiling with boxes and presided over by a big-bosomed Bubby. What I find is a spare, modern, chrome-and-glass store across from a Mercedes-Benz dealership. Miss Stevens is run by a crew of four very busy women.

I attempt self-service by looking through a rack of undergarments. The items hang in concave, waiting for the appropriate flesh-load to swell them into shape and give them meaning. There are tummy panels and underwires, dangling garters and contraptions intended for body parts I wasn't even sure I had. Until now, my lingerie repertoire has been straightforward: cotton bikini underpants, a few reliable bras, and a pair of thong panties for special occasions. The fact is, I wouldn't know a Merry Widow from a Black Widow.

I again look to see if anyone can help me, but all the salesladies are busy with other customers. One is buying an arsenal of nursing bras. She is sleek and well-groomed. This woman, I surmise, must have a baby somewhere, but it is nowhere in evidence. She gets her Coach wallet out of her crisp little Kate Spade bag and I think, *Oh, she has a nanny.*

I feel frayed and slouchy in my cutoffs and t-shirt. Looking down at my feet, I am suddenly horrified by my toes. Here it is, mid-June, and I am in Beverly Hills without a pedicure! How is it that I have managed to let myself go like this? I try to make myself disappear, but instead I only seem to grow larger. I tug self-consciously at my t-shirt, which seems to be riding up over my now massive Pussy Belly.

Handing the woman her receipt and her bag, the saleswoman turns her attention to me. She is an ample Hispanic woman in her mid-thirties. She has an air of focused practicality.

"Hello, I am Isabel. What do you need?"

"I think, maybe . . . a girdle." I wait a moment for her to notice how young and slender I really am and talk me out of it. But all she says is, "What kind?"

"Uh, I don't know. Something for my tummy, I guess . . . and maybe my tush."

"Do you have the dress with you?"

"Yes." I proffer the plastic Ralph's grocery bag that holds my ball gown.

She withdraws the dress and spreads it out on the glass counter, running a practiced hand over the fabric. It is then that I realize what cheap goods my dress really is. The fabric is the kind of cheesy polyester that would snag a hangnail if Isabel's French manicure weren't so flawless.

"Okay," she says, in a way that sounds like this is going to be a duck shoot, "let's try an all-in-one on you."

Moving to a rack on the back wall, she chooses what looks like a Kong-sized Ace Bandage. Then she leads me to a sumptuously appointed dressing room. "Be sure you pull this all the way up," she instructs me before closing the door.

I climb out of my loose, comfortable clothes, and begin to pack my white meat into the beige sausage casing. When I am only halfway into it, Isabel taps on the door, then opens it before I have a chance to arrange myself. She steps into the small room and closes the door behind her.

"Pull it up. You have not pulled it up all the way." I do a quick squat-thrust and manage to yank the thing up until it splits my crotch and digs into my armpits.

"Yes, now please lift your breasts and place them into the cups."

"Huh?"

"Your breasts—pick them up and put them into the cups."

I reach down and hoist up my poor, suckled, flattened-out breasts and let them puddle in the brassiere cups.

"Good," Isabel declares with a satisfied nod. I behold myself in the mirror, crammed into support wear like somebody's Aunt Sadie.

"Well, what do you think?" Isabel asks.

"Uh, I dunno . . ." I begin, but my voice is coming out small and bent with tears. "It's a little more than I bargained for."

"What do you mean? It gives you a nice line."

I am so loath to displease Isabel. "Oh, it's great, but isn't it a little *extreme?*"

"Put on the dress." Isabel commands, and I obey. The dress slides over my artificially sleekened form like silk on marble. I turn to the mirror. Under the triple-support, my Pussy Belly has been beaten into submission. The magic is back. I am the Candy Girl once more.

I execute a couple of coquettish spins, then sit down on the little pink tuffet in the corner. Immediately my air supply is cut off.

"Unghh, how do I breathe in this thing?!" I manage to gasp.

"You'll get used to it," Isabel reassures me.

The girdle cost twice as much as the dress.

Which is how I am here, seated at an outdoor banquet table, waiting for Patti Smith to start her set, struggling to breathe inside my support wear. Here beside the genuinely and righteously toned of Los Angeles, I feel armored in a lie. I hope nobody notices that I am breathing so shallowly and shivering slightly. The night air is chill across my bare shoulders and the polymers I am wearing offer no warmth. A breeze is blowing my fancy paper napkin, and for a moment I find myself missing Pussy Belly, for she was always good for anchoring a napkin to my lap.

The crowd begins to cheer as Patti enters and takes the microphone. She is a wraith in a vintage dress and army boots. This woman is beyond vanity; she is wholly engaged in art and wouldn't waste her energy on issues of flab or personal support. My heart sinks a little under my push-up bra. How have I come to this frivolous end?

Patty strums the opening chords of a song I recognize, but can't immediately identify. The tune takes me back to adolescence, when I was free and unfettered by sagging flesh and a creeping sense that the juicier part of my life is behind me.

The manufacturers of my rigid undergarment, anticipating how difficult it would be for a Party Girl to piddle while wearing their contraption, have thoughtfully installed an overlapping pee-flap at the crotch. Slowly, surreptitiously, I spread my legs under the banquet table and the vent opens. The soft night air dances across my exposed pussy and I suddenly feel giddy and free as a skinny-dipping teenager on a summer's eve.

"Ain't it strange?" Patti sings, and I'd have to agree that it is.

Falternamom

A variety-pack of Alterna-Moms bounces onto the stage. Dressed in baggy overalls, ripped fishnets with dyed, dread-locked hair, these are the Hip Mama Radical Cheerleaders. They line up and begin to chant,

> *"Our babies like to walk, our babies like to crawl,*
> *Our babies like to breastfeed and that's not all!"*

Each cheer is choreographed in faux drill-team fashion, their pompoms their clenched fists.

"Our babies go to protests, our babies change the world,
Our babies rewrite what it is to be a boy or a girl."

One mom, a butch dyke with a buzz cut and pendulous, braless breasts, pounds the floor rhythmically with her Doc Martens. On "girl," she and her squad spin around and yank down their pants, mooning the world.

I am at the second annual Mama Gathering, a colloquy

of radical feminist moms who have come together to the LAX Radisson for a weekend of workshops, potluck dinners, readings, and the chance to bond with other women who share their values, as well as their fondness for skin art, lunchbox purses and flannel. I am there covering the event for an alternative weekly I sometimes contribute to, so my alt. credentials are in order.

These are my people. Ideologically speaking, I fit in. I am, on paper, an alternative mom. I believe in what they believe: equal rights, the First Amendment, the right to whip out a tit and nurse my baby wherever and whenever her hunger strikes. I oppose big business, Republicans, moms who spank their children, hormones in milk. I believe in honoring my children's feelings and opinions and have "unschooled" them both. But compared to these righteous womyn I am a mere dabbler, a sham, a fake, a Falternamom. I am unable to go the dogmatic distance in the world of third-wave feminist motherhood. Why? I don't have the energy or the commitment to conform to the rigors of a fully alternative lifestyle. It's too much work and not enough sugar.

Modern, urban motherhood, it seems, is divided into two camps: traditional, mainstream mothers who swear by time-outs and convenience foods, Cartoon Network, and Ferberizing. The other camp is the alternative lifestyle moms, the doula-assisted, renewably resourced, politically correct moms. Trad-Moms read labels for caloric content, Alterna-Moms read labels for potential toxins. Trad-moms schedule C-sections and pedicures for the same day, Alterna-moms labor earnestly in their own beds, or in tubs of warm water. Trad-moms tuck their babies into deeply carpeted, color-coordinated nurseries and leave them there among the formaldehyde-off-gassing, pressed-wood furniture to cry themselves to sleep. Alterna-moms nurse their children to sleep in the family bed, swaddled in sheepskin, until they leave for college. Trad-Moms put their toddlers on leashes at Disneyland, while Alterna-Moms strap their young to their bodies and hike them up mountains.

When my children were first born I was filled with the giddy zeal that comes from realizing I could do the opposite of what my own parents did. Though my childhood home was liberal and intellectual, it was also pretty traditional. I was formula-fed and taught to mind my Ps and Qs along with my ABCs. As a new mother I wanted to break free of the conformist, oppressive mode of child-rearing that had so bummed me out in my youth. I began with cloth diapers.

I signed up with a venerable diaper service and had stacks of nappies delivered to my home. I purchased several nifty Velcro diaper wraps in baby-pleasing colors. I learned the appropriate diaper origami for newborns and in no time had my baby wrapped like a falafel to go in organic cotton. I felt pleased with myself for my conscientious stewardship of the earth's precious resources.

Things went swimmingly in those first, dewy, colostrum-filled days. My baby's tasteful smears were accommodated nicely by the diapers, and the novelty of diapers and all they contained had me enthusiastically changing at the slightest gurgle from below.

This went on for about a month, in which time I realized that every time my child peed, which was at least three times an hour, I would have to change her immediately or a nasty rash would occur.

Then one day I was caught out in the world with a wet baby and no clean diapers. I bummed a Huggy off another mom at the park and guiltily strapped my daughter into it. That diaper lasted six hours. It was a frikkin' miracle. I decided I would capitulate to convenience just the teensiest, weensiest bit and use disposables at night, if only to have a shot at sleeping through one.

It's a slippery slope down into the landfill. Nighttime disposables carried over into the day. The cloth diapers were good for many things: staunching a leaky boob, shoulder guards for spit-up, wiping up spills, but they never again saw my baby's butt. By Franny's six-month birthday, I had cancelled the Dydee Diaper Service with the rationale that all that diaper washing was polluting our nation's waterways, anyway.

That kind of fuzzy logic would last about two seconds at the Mama Gathering. These were earth mamas, women who had given their children names like "Skye" and "Gaia." Women for whom environmental commitment extended beyond asking for paper over plastic at the supermarket.

Aside from my pathetic diaper experiment, my parenting methods were pretty traditional. When Franny was a baby I sought out Mommy-and-Me groups at the local mall, thinking it would be networking . . . with kids! But it turned out to be sitting on the floor, rolling a ball back and forth with your toddler (which was exactly what we'd been doing at home) while other trad-moms droned on about tantrums and transitional objects. I became aware that my mothering techniques were maybe a little sub-par. These moms already had their babies' names on the waiting lists of several prestigious schools. I wasn't even playing Beethoven in the nursery. I wasn't showing my baby stimulating black-and-white images. I didn't even own a Diaper Genie for fucksake. In fact, I was the dysfunctional Diaper Genie, letting them pile up on the floor of my car when I changed Franny on the backseat.

While I enjoyed the handy tips, the fresh air, and the camaraderie of the other mommies, I felt like I was not in their league. I was too disorganized, too sloppy, too unprepared. I was always bumming snacks and mooching wipes off of them. I hadn't taken the time to paint puffy little white clouds on the ceiling of my daughter's room, as practically every other mother had. I had little interest in the "please" and "thank you" drills of traditional parenting. I used inappropriate language around my impressionable children, and was given to a certain amount of selfish crankiness.

As soon as Franny was old enough I decided to partake of the pleasures of preschool. I toured a number of places, both traditional and alternative. I visited schools where the wee mites were expected to sit quietly in a circle listening to stories, fully potty trained and asking for permission to prove it. I wanted my toddler to spend her days pursuing her own interests, as I certainly planned to be once she was out of the house.

This is how I fell in with the Alterna-Moms. The Mountain School was a fifty-year-old alternative school, located a mere half-mile from my house. After having seen countless behavior charts, tidy classrooms, searing asphalt playgrounds, and time-out corners, The Mountain School seemed like heaven. Built in a converted house, it was hippie-deluxe. Comfy, worn, donated furniture lined the walls, making it feel like home. At last I had found a community of moms who knew how to think outside the sandbox. The Alterna-Moms were artistic, forward-thinking, and free-spirited. They questioned everything, and thought through all their actions and reactions. They made solid, responsible choices concerning their children, the environment, their community, and their bodies.

I wanted desperately to fit in. I got to work, learning to use "I-messages" and the lingo of humanistic parenting. I had "special times" and "moosh plans" with Franny, and learned how to pack a sugar-free snack and lunch. When she got tired and overcranky, instead of saying, "You're tired, you need a nap," I would say, "Is your body telling you it's tired? Does it need a nap?" I wore baby Georgia in a sling, trying not to be alarmed by the unnatural way her neck bent in it. I even tried using cloth diapers again, until one exploded, leaking into the sling, and then into my blouse, so I furtively went back to disposables.

Being an Alterna-mom was a lot of work. It meant grinding up baby food and washing mud-stained clothes in scentless, non-sudsing, environmentally friendly soap. It meant driving out of my downscale 'hood over to the Whole Foods (or "Whole Paycheck," as my friend Lou calls it) in Beverly Hills to buy overpriced, organic food that my kids were too sugar-corrupted to palate. I stocked up on Sucanot and soy milk, which festered, uneaten, in my pantry.

I tried letting my kids eat when they were hungry and sleep when they were tired, but that just ended up making me overtired and fat. I was too self-conscious for role-playing, more interested in pot than hemp, and unwilling to give up the luxury of using the TV as a babysitter. While Alterna-Kids played richly imagined games with little more than bedsheets and cardboard boxes, mine lived in a drift of Barbie clothes and Bratz dolls. In the end, I sucked at Alterna-Momming. I simply didn't have the conviction required to actually stuff a birthday piñata with raisins and string cheese. I could talk the talk, but I couldn't walk ten feet in their Birkenstocks.

Realizing that I didn't fit in with the Traditional Moms or Alternative Moms, I felt lost, unmoored, alone in my lack of convictions. I was just a Slacker Mom with a guilty conscience.

After coming to this realization, it wasn't long before I found myself rebelling against the rebels. I brought sugar cookies to a sugar-free school bake sale (where they sold like hotcakes!). I got busted by a teacher for putting Go-

Gurts into my kids' lunch boxes. At the school bazaar I set up a Wedding Booth, offering traditional white weddings to the love children of "partnered," same-sex parents. I found I enjoyed the subversion. I became a wolf in unbleached cotton clothing.

I am feeling no less lupine here at the 2003 Mama Gathering, where the menu of workshops is a smorgasbord of free thought. With sessions that include anti-racist parenting, creative activism, alternative family health, sustainable living, 'zines and alternative media, and erotic writing, the vibe is one of simmering rage mixed with bitter resentment toward all things corporate and/or institutional. Caucasian moms share their anguish over their "white skin privilege" and seek out ways to empower their own racially mixed children. Humanistic educators espouse the virtues of child-led curricula. Anarchist moms express frustration with bringing their children to un-family-friendly political protests and vow to create actions with child care. Amongst all this angst and earnestness, I feel Ivana Trumpesque, a plastic poseur.

As I wander from panel to panel, I feel more and more alien. I agree with these people in principle on everything. I love their energy, their spirit, their collective "fuck you" to The Man. After all, I was an anarchist back in high school. I stole *Steal This Book*. What is it that is making me feel so ornery?

Maybe it's because being an Alterna-Mom is such a lifestyle choice, and that's finally where I always fall off the beam. "Life-Stylers" rankle me. People lacking in imagination about themselves sign up for lifestyles. Whether the theme is Urban Cowboy, Church Lady, Sex-Positive Swinger, Harley Dude: these lifestyles seem to come with wardrobe, ideology, and upholstery swatches so you don't have to make any difficult choices. All these Alterna-Moms would claim to be square pegs, misfits, rebels, and yet there's a feeling of mindless conformity here. Twenty-first-century rebellion today comes with a uniform: tattoos and vintage dresses, chunky shoes, hair dyed blue/black and shorn into blunted bangs and bobs. Nose rings and vibrators as accessories. What was the difference between that and a Brooks Brothers suit, or gang colors, or any of the other accoutrements that we use to identify ourselves? After six years of living among the alternative hiperati, I saw that these cookies had all been cut with the same shape. It depressed me. It made me feel bitchy.

I go to check out a "child-led curriculum" workshop, led by the director of our former preschool. Julie, a gentle, soft-spoken soul with salt-and-pepper hair and impossibly delicate hands, describes her school, where children are honored and get to make their own decisions, resolve their own conflicts, and are free to express all of their feelings. As she speaks I look around the room, watching moms with their preschool-aged young wriggling in their laps, tugging on their nipples. The moms' eyes are shining with excitement as mine once had. *Yes!* I wanted to shout, *Children should be honored and heard. But beware the cost!* I could see these children after a few years of child-centric education: muddy, unable to read, tantruming in the yard, telling their mothers to go fuck themselves, having their every feeling validated, no matter how shitty. It made me shudder.

I burst out of the room and head over to a brainstorming session in "creative activism," which yields ideas such as silk-screening political logos for onesies, making politically correct coloring books for kids, or using corporate, postage-paid envelopes to mail bricks back to the company. All these good ideas fill me with inertia. Have I become too cynical for political action? Too complacent? Or just too tired?

Toward the end of the creative activism session, Inga Muscio, author of *Cunt,* pipes up, "Chicken!" Huh? We all look to her for clarity. "Rotting chicken really stinks. Go to Wal-Mart and hide little pieces of chicken all over the store." It is brilliant, simple, inexpensive. A mom with two kids and a small baggie would never be noticed. She could easily mine the store with tiny pieces of toxic gristle, planting it amongst the flip-flops and flatware. But that mom probably wouldn't be me. Sure, I hate Wal-Mart as much as everyone else, but why take it out on the poor Wal-Mart shopper? Why expose the uninsured children of the broke and bargain-besotted to salmonella? Besides I won't do it because there aren't any Wal-Marts conveniently located near my home. It'd just be too much of a schlep to get to one.

Chicken is definitely not on the menu at the Mama Gathering, as it is a vegan event. Radisson Hotel policy prohibits serving brought-in lunches to the group, so we all sneak up to the fifth floor at noon for an under-the-radar bag lunch. I eat my hummus/veggie sandwich and drink my Soy-Um while secretly longing for a nice lamb kabob and a Coke.

As I watch the Mamas peel oranges and slip handfuls of Pirate's Booty to their kids, I realize that I have essentially been corrupted by my own mother, who raised me on Pepperidge Farm white bread and Lucky Charms.

Compared to my mother, I'm just a love bead away from being a total hippie. She is of the "quit your whining" school of parenting and holds a thinly veiled disdain for children and their noisy antics. Perhaps my whole yen for the Alterna-World came not from wanting to rebel against The Man, but simply against The Mom.

In spite of my disagreement with my mother's disciplinary methods, I sometimes find myself slipping into them like a pair of old Levi's. Being a conscientious parent is time consuming, and sometimes reasoning with intractable toddlers feels utterly pointless. I would allow myself to cut corners and say things like, "Because I said so!" It's just easier to stalk off, slam a door, lay down the law, give a time-out, than it is to negotiate, mediate, and work through whatever problems are dogging your kid.

After lunch, I wander out to the pool where Mamas swizzle their naked, uncircumcised tots around in the water, cooing to them over their tongue studs. My own lack of tattoos and piercings (if not my Aerosoles) mark me as a tragically Trad-Mom. What would they think of me if they knew I was raising my kids in a two-parent, middle-class household? That I owned a stack of Disney videos? That I immunized my kids and wore an underwire bra? That rather than a mind filled with dreams of a green, equitable future, I had a head stuffed full of amalgam fillings and dirty limericks?

The Mama Gathering has wound up with a party at a Veteran's Memorial Auditorium. Ariel Gore reads from her new book, and we are entertained by our own children who are given free access to the stage and a variety of musical instruments to jam with. One raven-haired, five-year-old boy straps on a junior-sized electric guitar and plugs into a tiny amp, letting loose with a searing, atonal guitar solo. All the Mamas swoon. Then we watch the Radical Cheerleaders take the stage to bring it on home,

> *"Our babies are our futures and our future's looking brighter,*
> *'cause each baby makes a woman a Mama and a fighter!"*

Too tired to fight, I gather up my babies and go home.

Journey to Another Girl

Kathleen picks me up at my house for our evening out. My daughters are bathed and in their pajamas. "Where are you guys going?" they ask.

"Oh, just out for a drink," I say, kissing their damp, fragrant heads. I blow a kiss to my husband and we head out into the night. We are off, not for Cosmos and girl talk, but to a West L.A. strip club to get lap dances.

We go to our usual place, 4Play on Cotner, located so close to schools and shopping that coming here feels like running an errand. As we pull up to the valet, I reflexively check my lipstick in the rearview mirror. Years of going out have trained me to prepare myself to meet the male gaze. But tonight the tables are turned and I will be the one appraising women's looks. The only looks I get here are ones of curiosity, like the one the valet gives me as I hand him my keys. I wonder how many station wagons he parks with booster seats and OUTSTANDING STUDENT OF THE MONTH bumper stickers.

I always feel a little nervous coming here, like I'm getting

away with something. Though Kathleen and I are not officially breaking any rules, we are definitely fucking with the
code. Middle-aged mothers don't go to strip bars on week-
nights. We should be home reading bedtime stories to our
daughters, doing the dinner dishes, making nutritious bag
lunches for tomorrow. A bouncer holds open the door for
us and I feel a giddy rush of excitement as I step into the
gentlemen's club.

The 4Play vibe is kind of English Country meets Z Gal-
lerie. Picture Ralph Lauren hip-deep in Victoria's juicy Secret. The decor is louche, plush, and just a little bit naughty.
Heavy burgundy velvet drapes hang like swollen labia from
the doors and walls. The palette is all deep reds and gold.
Over the bar a series of plastic, female bodies hang like
hunting trophies. They are headless and legless and have
only arms and hands to clutch at themselves in randy bas-
relief. They look like pervy mannequins that got kicked out
of Bloomingdale's window for misbehavior. One of them
lies draped across the bar like erotic road kill.

It is early in the evening and many tables are still empty.
Kathleen and I choose one on the far side of the stage. As I
unwind my scarf from around my neck, the dancer onstage
removes her bikini top. I catch a guy two tables over staring
at us, and he quickly looks away.

A redhead in a bustier comes over to take our order.
"Good evening, I'm Rose. Can I get you a drink? We're all
nude, so we don't serve alcohol here." Male chemistry
never ceases to amaze me in its simplicity. Down the street
at a panty bar called Plan B (a name I love, implying that
Plan A was to actually *get laid*), the guys are knocking back
Screwdrivers and watching girls dance around in their G-
strings with no problem. But add a shot of live pussy to the
mix and the situation gets instantly combustible. We order
chamomile tea.

The 4Play stage is bare but for the burnished, vertical brass pole. On that pole, spinning like a flesh-and-blood whirligig, is, of course, a naked girl. She has her leg hooked around the pole and she swings off it in a silky arc, her back arched, her bottle-blond, blunt-cut ends sweeping the buffed floor.

The dancer's overstuffed breasts shine under the klieg lights. This girl is pure stripper, all hair extensions and over-drawn lips. As she dances, pantomiming sex from behind, on top, missionary-style, the men get up from tables and move to the tip rail that rims the stage to get a closer look. Her pussy is neatly shaven, flawless, and looks as though it were sculpted of latex, not flesh. It is a textbook cunt.

Though Kathleen and I are the only female patrons, be-tween the dancers, the hostess, the bartender, and the wait-resses, the women outnumber the men, and they are definitely the ones calling the shots. The sexual behavior code is clearly defined and enforced here: look, don't touch. It applies to all females and it liberates us from the stress of having to draw boundaries.

Rose brings us our chamomile tea with lemon and honey, which is exactly what I'd be drinking if I were at home. Prohibition is another thing that makes strip joints such a lovely place for ladies to hang out. There are no drunks to pester you. This feels like the calm eye of the male sexual storm that rages outside in the world. Everywhere else, men are making passes, wolf-whistling, leering at and harassing women in bars, fueled by booze and acute horni-ness. But here the men are calm, their sober attention fo-cused intently on the appropriate target—the dancer onstage.

The G-string-clad dancer is having a Narcissus moment in the mirror, fondling herself and getting off on her reflec-tion. She presses her breasts into the glass, pushing out her ass. Her fake breasts ridge and shine bizarrely from the pressure and look as though they might pop.

"Ouch," Kathleen says with a grimace.

"I know. That's gotta hurt." The dancer turns around, hoists a boob, and suckles herself.

"Is it even possible to nurse a baby with those?" I ask Kathleen.

"It depends on whether the implant was done under the pectoral muscle or not." My friend is a painter of nudes and married to a doctor. She knows her anatomy.

"Well, at least her breasts won't sag from nursing."

"Not necessarily. Nursing compromises the Cooper muscle," Kathleen informs me, lifting her arm and pointing to the muscle running alongside her own nicely-shaped breast. "The Coopers are droopers."

This makes me guffaw, and I draw the gaze of several men. What must they be thinking of us? Do they take us for lesbians? Kathleen is dressed in a long, flowing skirt, her straight, brown hair loose around her shoulders. She has a soft voice and a slow, gentle way of moving. She would be the femme. There's no doubt that I, with my throaty laugh and pointy boots, am the butch.

I am not a lesbian, but it's not the first time I've been mistaken for one. I did my *pro forma* lesbian thing back in college when I slept with my roommate for a semester. But that was at Sarah Lawrence, where lesbianism is treated like a work-study program—"Junior Year On A Broad," you could call it. I had sex with Lina like I was taking an exam, filling in all the dots evenly, hoping for a good grade. After a few well-meaning but alien encounters, I found I missed guys. I missed their funky smells, their stiff cocks, and their bad attitudes. Most of all, I missed their *otherness*. After that, I went back to men for good.

I am not immune to the beauty of women, but it is the same attraction I feel for luxury cars: I can see that they are beautiful, I appreciate the work that goes into making them, but I have no real urge to drive one. I certainly wouldn't want to *own* one. But I like to look at them, run my fingers along their sleek curves, sink into their upholstery, and inhale their scent. I like women's curb appeal.

A leggy brunette in lacy bra and panties comes to our table and leans into us. "Hi," she says, smiling and offering a long-fingered hand to shake, "I'm Alexis." Alexis has a broad, wholesome smile and shiny Breck-girl hair. What's your name?"

"I'm Erika," I say, shaking her shapely hand with my bitten mitt. "This is Kathleen." Alexis puts her little purse up on our table and pulls up a chair. A gentleman would have offered her a seat, I reprimand myself.

"So, is this your first time here?" she asks in a pleasant, So-Cal twang.

"Actually, no," Kathleen says, "we've been here before."

"Oh really?" Alexis says with a raised eyebrow. "You're regulars?" I look to Kathleen to maybe run with the conversational ball, but she is untalkative tonight so I jump in.

"Well . . . this is only my second time here."

"Oh, what other clubs have you been to?" Alexis asks brightly, like we're talking about shopping malls.

"Crazy Girls on La Brea and Star Strip on La Cienega."

"Oh, how is Crazy Girls?"

"Actually, I thought it was a little seedy."

"Oh? Yeah, well, most places aren't as nice as this."

In my own limited sampling of strip clubs, I'd have to agree with her. 4Play is indeed the aesthetic exception to the rule. Most places are a cheesy assemblage of flat, black paint, smoked mirrors, and rope lights. Slatternly girls dance in pits, rimmed by a bar of leering customers. Worst of all, the lap dance areas at these other clubs are just big rooms banked with couches, making it more of a mosh pit than a private place.

We embark on some girl talk. Alexis tells us she likes to shop for her costumes in tonier stores, and we all agree that Frederick's of Hollywood has nice stuff these days and we love the Victoria's Secret sales, but their stuff doesn't last as long and blah, blah, the conversation winds in small, ordinary circles.

A male voice purrs over the P.A., "That was Kyra, everybody. Open up your wallets for Kyra." Kyra crawls on her hands and knees to gather the bills men have thrown onto the stage. The business of boners involves a lot of subjugational body language on the part of its workers. There was a time when it set my teeth on edge, when I railed at every sexist ad and double standard. Now one of the thrills in coming here is the moral tension it creates in me. Who really has the power here, the men or the women? Am I boldly taking control of my sexuality, or knuckling under a male standard?

I like to think it's the former, but I fear feminism got stalled at sexual power. Women claim their sexuality as though it were some big coup, when really it's just a basic human right, coupled with a cultural loosening of the sexual codex. Sexual power is merely the bottom rung on the ladder of social influence, well below financial and political power. When I see sisters claim sexual power and nothing else, it makes me sad.

"Well, you let me know if you want a dance," Alexis says, sensing Kathleen and I are not yet ready for our lathering up. She's moving on to hotter prospects. I feel a pang of guilt, because it's true. Alexis is too wholesome and friendly for my purposes. I'd hire her to babysit my kids, but not to give me a lap dance. She is simply not my type. Do men ever feel this kind of guilt when rejecting a lap dancer?

* * *

The dancers who are not onstage are circulating around the room. There is a black girl in a leopard-print bikini, a Latina with hoop earrings and hair down to her waist, an Asian beauty in smoky eye makeup. It's an erotic Epcot Center.

Our household budgets allow Kathleen and me a mere two dances each tonight. We want to continue looking, talk to a couple more girls before we buy.

It is fun to shop for girls. That I am playing into the objectification of women is perfectly clear, and though it makes me uneasy, it doesn't stop me. In a culture where every other girl has a tattoo on her ass and a stud in her tongue, getting hung up on the politics of lookism feels as quaint and pointless as using a turn signal at an empty intersection; you would be alone and irrelevant in your principles.

The challenge of choosing a dancer lies in the fact that these girls were not created with my aesthetics in mind. They have been grown in the petri dish of male desire, and they are pale and moist as mushrooms that have never seen sunlight. Like any purebred, they have a strangely mutant quality. Their prizewinning traits are accented—tits, hair, lips, ass—while less important traits become recessive—irony, point of view, sense of humor, hands that can pry the lids off of pickle jars.

My mojo tends to center on intangibles. What attracts me to men is personality, not pectorals. I like a man with a point of view, an esoteric hobby, a sense of humor. I like boxer guys, not Speedo guys. Among the many intangibles that drew me to my husband was the careful way he held guitars and the fact he could bake a pie from scratch.

I don't hold women to the same standard. Which is why I, a heterosexual woman, am here, and not at Chippendale's, even though they are essentially the same product. Chippendale dancers have the sex appeal of chipmunks. If I am to consume a corporate sex product, I would rather it be female. Why am I so much more willing to accept a lady stripper as sexy than a guy in a weenie-sling? Have I simply been shaped by our sexist culture to have some kind of Pavlovian response to hot chicks?

So what am I looking for tonight? Well, that's part of the fun. Sometimes on long airplane flights I play a game with myself. I page through the Sky Mall catalogue with its endless array of absurd offerings—the Barnoculars and massage boots, the deerskin driving caps and golf bag drink caddies, the endless, pointless detritus of our consumer culture. The game is that I *have* to pick one item off each page. Which is the most inoffensive product? Which one could I possibly imagine living with? I look for the object that might have some relevance to my life, like the bottomless cat feeder or the sonic steamer. These things not only might have some useful application, but also wouldn't make me feel alien to myself. Picking out a naked dancer feels like the same game. I look for the girl that most closely resembles someone I might fall in love with. Someone I could see sitting in my living room. Someone interesting, someone who might make me laugh.

The faceless emcee croons, "And now, folks, let's bring to the stage that lovely vixen . . . Ava!"

The lights change, as does the music. The syntho-pop beat is replaced with the lickety-split strum of a guitar. A blonde with a retro, Rita Hayworth-style, peroxided updo sails onstage. She is dressed in strappy pumps, a fetching teddy, and is draped in a diaphanous, boa-trimmed boudoir duster. Her lips are painted hot red and her skin is creamy white. The song she is dancing to is by the Squirrel Nut Zippers, and she's doing a kind of swing strip. Here is a girl with an idea or two, I think admiringly. She pivots up onto the pole with astonishing grace and strength, and wraps her legs around it, spiraling slowly down. I catch my breath. This girl is powerful. She has clearly put a lot of time and thought into her act. Kathleen and I exchange a look.

"She's hot!" Kathleen says.

"She's mine," I reply. It's not just that she's pretty. It's not just that she's cool. It's the music. The swingy guitar reminds me of my husband, himself a guitar player formerly of a swing band. He's probably out in our garage right now, playing a similar riff. She's got a Marlene Dietrich-meets-Mae-West vibe. Doug has a weakness for cool blondes. He'd want me to go for her. There is a strange crossover between my desire for my man at home and my desire for this woman that creates a circuit in my libido. For the first time this evening, I feel a jolt of arousal.

When the song ends, Ava collects her underwear and her tips and exits. I watch the stage door anxiously for her to reappear. She does, and I flag her over to our table.

"Hi," she says with a sultry smile. "Would you like a private dance?"

"Yes, please," I say, getting up. She leads me to a room in the back of the club. In it is a series of stalls with chairs. The song is still playing, a techno-dance version of "Maneater," over the P.A., and since songs time lap dances, we make idle chit chat as we wait to start.

"I loved your act."

"Oh, thanks."

"It was very original."

"Well, I try to have fun with it."

I am nervous around Ava, and not sure what to say next, so she asks, "Are you straight, gay, or bi-curious?"

"I don't know. I guess I'm just curious."

I hate the word "bi-curious." I don't mind if people think I'm attracted to women, but I don't want them to think I'm some kind of "swinger." It's not that I wouldn't enjoy sex with some other people. But honestly, who? Friends are utterly out of the question, as I value my friendships too much to literally fuck them up. That leaves strangers. Once I checked out a Web site for a swingers' club in Tarzana. The photo-tour revealed room after converted room of carpet-covered orgy platforms. It looked like a massive kitty condo. I pictured pale, freckled hands with red-lacquered nails clawing at the pile in ecstasy. One photo featured a large deli tray set out on a buffet table next to a sliding glass door. Among festoons of parsley, the edges of the baloney were curling in the late afternoon sun. This is what I think of when I think of anonymous sex with strangers.

The song finally ends, and Ava drops a token in the box at our feet. The next song starts up, "Independent Women" by Destiny's Child. I know this song from the *Charlie's Angels* soundtrack which my daughters dance to at home. I push the thought of my children out of my mind as Ava straddles my lap and gets to work. She rolls her hips and slides her hands over my body. At first I just watch as she does this to me. It is interesting to be this close to this kind of person. She is as perfect in close-up as she is from a distance. Her skin is soft as velour. I can see no sign of blemish or blackhead. How do these girls do it? It's not so much that they are made of plastic, as they seem to have been dipped in it.

I wonder if men are able to appreciate the craft of beauty. Do they notice the perfectly tweezed eyebrow, get turned on by a beautiful earring or a silky garment the way I can? My sex stands around in stores caressing silks and four-hundred-thread-count sheets. We buy bath beads and scented candles. "Softness" is an erotic mandate for women, and there is little that is softer than Ava.

My powers of observation begin to ebb as Ava works on

me slowly. Libido trumps rationality when another human being is running her lips over your neck. She breathes into my ear and trails her hands down to my hips, pressing her fragrant breasts into me. The flutter in my groin quickly becomes a full-on beating of hooves, and I start moaning a little, grinding her back.

Lap dances are perfect for housewives. It's all foreplay. There is no expectation of returning sexual favors, or of climax. We don't have to do much work. Also, it seems to me that the physical possibilities between two women in a lap dance setting are more favorable. Men don't get the benefit of breast-on-breast action, and while I don't have a boner to grind, Ava effectively compensates by pressing her thigh between my legs. Girls know what girls like, and Ava has hit my polka dot. I start moaning into her ear, "Sweet, sweet."

I am cognizant of the house rules, so I keep my hands to myself, but she moves my hands onto her ass, and I stroke her like a cat, and she purrs back at me. I have a feeling the rules are more easily bent by female customers. The nonthreat works both ways. Ava lets me run my tongue over her shoulder and flick at her nipple. The beefy guard at the door of the dance room pays no attention. Ava tugs at my stretchy top, exposing my bra. She reaches down into it and strokes my breast, which causes me to again croon into her ear, "Oh, sweet, sweet . . ."

I am fully in touch with my inner strumpet now, and it is like meeting an old friend. There were times, before I married, when I would indulge in sex for its own sake. It wasn't always about love, or infidelity. It was just about the simple pleasure of bodies discovering each other. This feels like that, and it brings me back to my old self, as it simultaneously frees me from who I am now.

Desire changes its shape over a lifetime. In the middle of

mine I have come to see that compared to love, lust is almost chaste in its simplicity. It wants what it wants, and you either feed it or suppress it. I want to be touched.

The song ends too soon, so I stay for another. When that one is over, I long for one more. But this is how they get you. I have reached my financial limit for the evening, and I pull myself away from Ava. I've gotten what I came for, and it's not like this is going anywhere. We stand up and rearrange ourselves before picking up our purses and exiting the booth. I return to the table to find Kathleen waiting for details.

"How was it?" she asks.

"Divine," I say, sitting down and taking a swig of cold tea.

"Then I'm going for it, too." Kathleen flags down Ava and disappears into the back room with her.

As I sip the dregs of my tea, I feel very different. I am tingling, alive, centered. I think of all the money women spend on pedicures and facials, body scrubs and reflexology. I wonder if we wouldn't all be better off just getting a lap dance. The strip club is a kind of spa for the mojo. Fifty bucks gets you two dances, a soothing cup of tea, and leaves you feeling sexually recharged.

A redhead in pigtails, knee socks, and a crotch-length pleated skirt does a dirty schoolgirl pole dance, which reminds me this is a school night. I'd like to get home and give my husband a good rogering before I crash. My spouse doesn't have to come to the club (though that's good, too) to benefit. Just the idea of me being here turns him on. He will undoubtedly be up when I get home, waiting to reap the rewards of an equally stirred-up wife. Post-strip-bar sex is a special treat for longtime lovers.

* * *

Kathleen is gone for two songs and comes back looking a little sheepish. "I was going to dance with Alexis, but Ava was too good."

"I know, I had the same problem."

"Yeah, but I really swore to myself that I was going to dance with two different girls tonight. Why am I always monogamous in these places?"

"Well, Kathleen, I guess we are all creatures of habit, no less in titty bars than anywhere else in life," I reassure her.

"Let's go home," my friend says.

When I get home I find a note on the dining room table from Georgia. In her chunky scrawl she has written, *"Mommy, I missed you. I love you so . . . much. I can't stand it."* I smile at her use of the ellipses. Though only in first grade, she has somehow intuited that this punctuation will communicate her deep, inchoate longing for me. She wanted my body next to hers at bedtime. Tonight was hard for her. Her desires were sacrificed for my own. I suddenly see that this is the logical, if somewhat ironic, conclusion of my own erotic appetite: the creation of another girl who yearns to be held.

Bum Wrap

"MAH-MAY!" I pause, my fork mid-lift, a toothsome morsel poised for consumption. Then again, "MAAAAAAH-MAY!!" I can tell by the way my four-year-old daughter's voice shrilly rings off tile that she is summoning me from the bathroom. With a beleaguered sigh, I put down my fork and get up to go wipe her ass.

I open the door and am greeted by the winking brown eye of my youngest's bumhole. She is in her ready-to-be-wiped pose: downward-facing dog. As I ball up some toilet paper I begin my now-routine lecture.

"Georgia, you're a big girl now. It's time you started wiping your own tushy."

"I know, I know," she says, bored by this topic.

"Okay, here is the toilet paper. You do the first wipe and then I'll check you."

"No, you do it."

"But Georgie, if I do it you'll never get good at it." The stench from the bowl is reaching my nostrils and I can feel my appetite for lunch waning. I want to get this over with, so striking another blow for co-dependency, I wipe her ass and flush the toilet.

When I was pregnant with my first child, I was warned time and again about the drudgery of diaper changing. It was always cited, along with interrupted sleep, dirty laundry, and tantrums, as a low point of parenting. But I found that changing diapers was one of my favorite jobs. After all, what is more delightful than hoisting your baby onto the changing table and gazing into her clear-water blue eyes as you dab and daub her fragrant, dimpled flesh? It was a nice moment for engaging in some scintillating, one-sided dialogue. "Oh, it's a poopy diaper! Yes, it is! You're a super-pooper!" My baby would gurgle back at me in amused fascination. I loved the smell of powder and the opportunity to suck on tiny feet that kicked temptingly toward my mouth. It was a good opportunity for blowing raspberries on her rounded tummy while at the same time making a frank appraisal of her inoffensive digestive state.

The taupe-colored mole sauce of the breastfed baby is not in the least malodorous. Gradually, as solids are introduced, the contents of the diaper change. Yes, the smell gets stronger, but only marginally so, and it was always amusing to see whatever I had fed my baby come out whole on the other side. Diapers were a *déjà-vu*-like assemblage of peas, carrot cubes, and, once in a while, a Jackson Pollock spatter of color from a chewed-up crayon.

But once the baby starts walking and making her own broader, less wholesome dietary choices, then poop turns to shit and the party is over. The first time I realized that the smear of poo in a diaper, left unmolested, is, in fact, a long coil of turd, I decided I was ready to potty train.

Naturally, my toddlers were not. My firstborn, Franny, a champion pot-pisser by the age of two, waited until she was three and a half before she pooped in the potty. That was a year and a half of watching her peel off her underpants, strap on a Pull-up, and go into a corner to quietly and intently move her bowels. With my second child graduating to solids, I anticipated eagerly a day when I would not be up to my nose in dookie.

I begged Franny to just *try* pooping in the potty. I gave her potty books, bought her a squishy ring to sit on, and provided her with premoistened toddler towelettes. I reasoned with her, I cajoled her, then I threatened her and bribed her. All of my best parenting tools failed, and I began to resent my child for being so stubborn, so chicken, such . . . a child. Finally, one day at school her friend Noah, a late-blooming potty pooper himself, shared with her his own, recently conquered fear of letting one drop. He told her that he understood that it was scary, but that it would be okay—in fact, really good. This insight from a sage fully eight months her senior finally convinced her, and she never saw the inside of a diaper again.

Things were looking up for kid two and number two. Georgia got on the pot young and has always been a relaxed and productive pincher. But she balks at wiping herself. Is it fear? Stubbornness? Or is she just trying to keep me in the poop loop?

"Smoke a match, Mommy," my youngest commands. And I do, dropping the tiny flame into the toilet bowl with a hiss. It's been four years since Franny's bathroom breakthrough, and here I am, still in the crack trenches, washing somebody else's feces off my hands. I know some day, like magic, Georgia will emerge from the bathroom with a sparkling, self-cleaned anus, but who knows when that proud day will dawn? I dry my hands, check my aging reflection in the mirror, and shuffle back out to the dinner table to sit down to my cooling bowl of beef stew.

Sacred 'Grounds

It is late afternoon, as we finally pull into the parking lot at Veteran's Park. It's been a long day of housecleaning and Barney reruns and I can feel my bad mood pressing in on the backs of my eyeballs as I slide open the van doors and set my girls free. They escape with happy screeches.

I find a quiet bench to drink my to-go double latte and take a moment for myself. I realize crossly that I have left my magazine at home. I blame the children. *If they weren't so fucking needy, I might have a moment to think about myself.* Clearly I need desperately to revivify and relocate my sense of humor. Was it really only half an hour ago that I called out, *Who wants to go to the playground?* in a forced, singsongy voice?

"PlayGROUND! PlayGROUND!" the girls cried in unison, jumping up and down on the sofa, their pent-up energy making them a pair of blond pistons. Clearly, I wasn't the only one who needed to get out of the house.

"Okay, which park?"

"I want the Yellow Swing Park!" said Georgia.

"No, the Dinosaur Park!" countered Franny.

"Yellow Swing!!" Georgie yelled, digging her heels in.

The Yellow Swing Park is located on a quiet *cul de sac*. It features a nicely put-together play structure, a well-maintained restroom, and, most importantly for Georgia, the Yellow Swing. Hanging from the swing bar, next to the standard-issue, industrial rubber sling swing and baby bucket, is a deep, high-backed, injection-molded seat with armrests. Manufactured, I suspect, with the differently-abled child in mind, this is the La-Z-Boy of swings. A kid can really kick back, take a load off, *chill out* in this swing.

"The Yellow Swing Park works for me," I said, strapping the girls into their sandals and herding them toward the front door. I saw myself lollygagging on a blanket under one of the Yellow Swing Park's Jacarandas, with one eye on the kids, the other eye on the latest issue of *Bust Magazine*.

"*Noooo*, Mommy," Franny protested in a whine like a circular saw, slicing through my reverie. "We were just there with Daddy. I want the Dinosaur Park." She meant Roxbury Park, but renamed by us for the group of three large dinosaurs that stand near the west gate. They are brightly colored, unintimidating, and just the right size to be straddled by a pint-sized, Bronto-busting cowgirl. What makes the dinos magical, though, is the cool, prehistoric mist that rises from vents beneath their feet. The mist operates on a four-minute cycle, and I have seen children play in this unearthly fog until their clothes are wringing wet.

"I don't know, honey . . ." I had hedged. Though the Beverly Hills park is deluxe, it's also an awful lot of real estate over which to keep track of two kids. It's better to tag-team this park with another mom.

"The Dinosaur Park feels like too much work for me today, girls. Besides . . . Mommy really needs a coffee." Incredibly, there is no Starbucks adjacent to this park, and as my friend Mark says, in Los Angeles, it's all about regulating the dosage.

"How about the Prickly Park?" I offered, hoping for a compromise. The Prickly Park is in West Hollywood, conveniently located behind a coffeehouse that also sells banana-nut muffins the size of catcher's mitts.

"Yeah!" Franny enthused, sensing a sugar fix in her near future. "The Big Slide! The Big Slide! The Big Slide!"

The Big Slide is the Prickly Park's main attraction: a really, really tall, spiraling, tube slide. To get to the top of the ladder you must climb no fewer than fourteen steps. The ride down is turbo-shot and a lawsuit waiting to happen.

"No. I don't want the Prickly Park! I don't want it!!" Georgie cried, her body rigid in protest as I tried to buckle her into her car seat.

"Why not, Georgia? What's wrong with Prickly Park?" I said, my own voice notching upward. In a minute I am going to completely lose my shit. I will yell at them, make them shake in their sandals. Put them in therapy for the rest of their lives.

"Because," she replied, her lip quivering, her blue eyes spilling over with conviction, "it's *too prickly.*" She had me there. Instead of sand, the ground is covered in cedar chips which "prickle" their bare feet. Frankly, if my kids can't play barefoot they'd almost rather not play at all, and prickly feet would be just the thing to put my three-year-old right over the edge.

"Okay, okay, we won't go there." Georgie relaxed her body and I snapped her seat buckle. It wasn't yet 3:30, and we were already solidly into what a Mommy-and-Me gal pal once described as "the Arsenic Hours." Georgia was unraveling fast and I could feel a cable of stress tightening between my ears. Clearly we needed snacks if we were going to make it from now to dinner in one piece. I made a long-overdue executive decision, put the van in gear, and headed for a nearby Starbucks/Noah's Bagels combo which also happened to be on the way to ... the Yellow Brick Road Park. This park, located near the old Selznick Studios, features an Emerald City-esque play castle and a yellow spiral painted on the ground. The girls love to recreate Dorothy's first ruby-slippered steps while singing, "We're off to see the Wizzer, the wonderful Wizzer da Loz!"

Thanks to the restorative powers of the bagel smear, Georgia is now happily filling her empty Naked Juice bottle with sand while Franny has made friends with a girl on the seesaw. I catch a whiff of ocean in the cooling air. The late afternoon sun feels like a warm blanket across my back. The buzz from my latte kicks in and I feel a sudden swelling of relief to be out of the house, away from the phone and dust bunnies, the thousand little tasks that prevent me from just being still.

I watch a bed-headed, unshaven daddy pushing his round-faced little girl on a swing. He is speaking to her in a mix of Italian and English. They are playing a game where he pushes her from the front and then turns his back on her, pretending not to notice her swinging right back into him. She knocks him down with her feet and he does an elaborate *commedia* pratfall into the sand, sending the girl into peals of helpless laughter. The dad gets up, brushes himself off with mock indignation, and then does it all over again.

It dawns on me that this is the real magic of playgrounds. It has nothing to do with equipment, or locale. The fact is, children can play anywhere, but grownups often need playgrounds in order to play. We need to get away from our computers, put down our phones, shrug off our purses, and follow our kids down a rabbit hole or into a sandbox and start digging, pretending, playing. Playgrounds demand that we let go of our angst, our agendas, our selves.

Georgia comes running up to me and pulls me toward the swings. "Mommy, push me on the swing!"

"Okay!" I say, springing to my feet and following her over to an empty swing. She grabs the chains and hoists herself into the seat, hovering over it for a second like a gymnast on the rings, before she drops down into it. I give her a one-handed push.

"No, Mama, *Underdog!*"

"Are you sure?"

"Yes, Mama! Yes! Underdog!"

I step forward and grab the chains above her hands, stopping the swing. I lean into the chains and hoist her up as high as I can, my arms extended, my toes digging into the sand. She dangles in the air like a skier mid-lift, swaying gently. We both giggle with anticipation of what's next, savoring each other in this moment. "Now!" she finally commands, and I release the swing. She drops down with a jolt and swings back into a wide arc. "Heeeeee!!" she cries, and I come around to the front of the swing to watch as she swoops back toward me. Her baby hair is floating on the breeze, her wide smile mirrors my own.

Saving Sophie

Sophie has a voice like a dirt road. At three, she sounds like she's been smoking Camel straights for thirty years. It is one of many things I find endearing about her. It is close to dinnertime and all the kids are hungry. Sophie (my best friend's daughter and my daughter's best friend) is in the dining room eating some cut-up cantaloupe. It's just a quick snack to save her from melting down before her mom, Rae, takes her and her brother out for dinner. I am in the kitchen, washing the cutting board. In the next room I hear Rae ask her, "Sophie, are you okay? Sophie, are you choking?"

I wait to hear Sophie's husky reply. But Sophie, never at a loss for words, is silent. Rae's voice notches up an octave. "Sophie, ARE YOU CHOKING?!"

The verb "choking" implies some kind of sound and motion. As I run into the dining room, I'm struck by how little of either is coming from Sophie. Her mother scoops her up and pounds her on the back. Nothing. She tries to Heimlich her daughter, but still she is silent. Choking is a moment of suspended animation: time slows, then quickly wastes.

I, too, give Sophie a whack on the back. This has never not worked before and we keep hitting and shaking her. Gobs of cantaloupe come flying out of her mouth, but still there is no sound.

As we shake her harder, I can tell that this is not going anywhere. We are too unfocused. Precious seconds are ticking past. "Oh my God, what do we do?" Rae pleads, her voice a tightened piano wire of fear. I take Sophie from Rae, who crumples to the floor. The room chills. Death is in here with us, and Rae, a fatalist by nature, is accepting it. "Oh God, she's going to die."

Her words strike me as preposterous. *No one is dying here today,* I think, sticking my finger in Sophie's mouth and feeling around. I feel her tongue, her palate, her uvula. There is something soft and round at the back of her throat. Is that the melon, or a tonsil? The flesh of both is nearly identical to my sightless fingertip. But this thing is in the wrong place—it's got to be melon. I can touch it, but I can get no purchase on it. I pull my finger out.

What do I do? I don't want to push it further down. Should I stop? I pull out my finger and watch as Sophie's skin tone changes. Rae has begun keening, letting out an anguished wail. The room grows darker, and I wonder for a moment if this is the shutting down of life as we know it. *No,* I think, *it's late, it's dinnertime, it's tubby time! It's time to try again.*

Sophie's jaws are clamped shut. "Open up, Sophie!" I command, as I pry her teeth apart and reach in. I touch that soft mound again, and again and again, and I hope this poking at least will cause her to vomit and dislodge the melon. I push my big hand farther into her small mouth, and I extend my finger as far back as it possibly can go and then . . . I feel the tip of my nail dig into the soft flesh of the cantaloupe and I hook it and bring it up.

Sophie's voice escapes in a pained yowl; spit and blood run down her chin, and finally, a red glob, like a piece of blood orange, drops out of her mouth and lands on top of her pink suede, Blues Clues sneaker, which is lying on the floor.

"She's okay!" I announce in a singsongy voice that I hope will diffuse all our dread. Rae gathers her child up and presses her, gasping, into her body. She holds her as though she'd like to put her right back inside of her, where she knows it's safe. I look up to see my own children, agape and confused, staring at the bloody glob on Sophie's shoe.

"Sophie's bleeding," my own three-year-old daughter observes.

"I must've scratched her throat with my nail," I try to explain. I feel guilty, like I've hurt her friend needlessly. I grab a paper towel and quickly wipe up the evidence of my assault. This is my house, my cantaloupe, my fault. I bring Sophie a damp rag and wipe her face. I get her a drink of cool water. I wonder if Sophie will be afraid of me now. I say again, this time to Rae, "I really had to dig around in there. I'm afraid I scratched her throat with my fingernail."

I think about that fingernail. A lifelong nail biter, I had only recently found the self-restraint to let it grow. Just a thin, eighth-of-an-inch crescent of white had grown in over the past week. It dawns on me that had I still been biting my nails, Sophie might have died.

I sit down on the floor. My legs are quivering and can't hold me up. Rae is sitting on the floor, too, and incredibly, she is putting Sophie's shoes on. She had promised her kids dinner at Burger King, and if that is still the plan, then life must be going on. I am stunned by how quickly we shifted from ordinary, to extraordinary, and then back again. It all happened so fast I wonder if it happened at all. Rae stands Sophie on her feet and shuffles across the floor to me on her knees and throws her arms around me. "Thank you," she says. "Thank you for saving my daughter's life."

In terms of drama, saving a life outranks giving life. The miracle of birth is long and logical, dawning on you slowly, so that by the time your baby is in your arms it all seems perfectly right. But saving a life is much different; it's a flash of brinksmanship, an odd mixture of luck, guts, and stubborn denial.

Sophie's father, David, called later to thank me, but the words "thank you" and "you're welcome" belong to the etiquette of everyday life and felt awkward. While he struggled to express his gratitude, I tried to reckon with what I had learned about everyday life: that normalcy is nothing more than a silken curtain that hangs between us and death . . . which is always in the room. The curtain merely obscures death's presence so we don't lose our minds to fear. It's as though we are living in a perverse episode of *Let's Make a Deal;* at any time, Carol Merrill can pull back the curtain to reveal a lifetime supply of grief. In these moments either the instrument of salvation is on hand and functioning, able to yank the curtain shut again, or it isn't. It all had very little to do with me. In fact, rather than feeling heroic, saving Sophie made me see how helpless I really am.

For a moment I wondered why we dare take the chance of having children in the first place, when so much is at stake. But then, in the background of David's house I heard Sophie's gravelly little voice, calling out for her bedtime bottle, so we hung up and I went to kiss my children good night.

The Gift of the Magi

"Mommy, do we believe in God?" Franny asks me one day near Christmas, out of the blue. I want to tell her no, we do not believe in God, but we do believe in Santa Claus. But I can see my daughter is drawn toward God, searching for Him in her agnostic home life. I believe that anyone should be able to believe what they want, especially my own daughter, so I tell her, "I don't, but that doesn't mean that you can't."

When I tell my father later that Franny may well be a believer some day, he heaves a great sigh and says, "Oh Holy Hannah, have we all toiled in vain here?!"

I was raised by a pair of atheist writers, who taught me to put my faith in fiction. So naturally I knew the story of the Nativity. I could tell it like a fairy tale, from the Star of Bethlehem to baby Jesus asleep in the manger. Of course, being a city girl, I had no idea what a manger was. Like Sleeping Beauty's deadly spindle, my mental picture of this particular item was hazy, though I understood its importance in the narrative. I knew about the Three Kings bringing spices as presents. Spices? *Please*. Santa Claus brought Lincoln Logs and Barbie Dolls all the way from the north pole. To my mind, the Magi were low-end Santas at best.

In the first grade, right after Thanksgiving, my best friend Samantha and I were asked to play angels in the upper-school Christmas pageant. Like mangers, pageants were also an unknown quantity. From what I gathered, they were more than a play and less than a musical. Why Sam and I were chosen from all the other little angels in our first-grade class for this upper-school honor was equally mysterious. I thought Sam's mom had something to do with it, as she was Christian and put great store in our pageant participation.

Everything I knew about religion, I learned from Sam's family. When I slept over at her house on Saturday nights, her mom would stuff us into prickly church dresses Sunday morning and haul us off to services.

Going to church was like visiting a foreign country— strange and exotic. I loved how you could jump off a busy midtown street corner into the sudden, murky, cool stillness of a church, like diving into a pond. The squeak and whispers of people trying to be quiet made my skin tingle. I loved the scent of hot wax and wet wool that hung in the air. I loved the stories written in stained glass and the candles that you were actually allowed to light and make wishes on. Most of all I loved the crinkly, thin pages of the dolly-sized prayer books. Christianity was magic and I wanted *in*.

I thought being in the pageant was a good first step. Though Sam and I had no lines or stage business in the show, we were required to attend one rehearsal, in which we were arranged in a silent, beatific tableau around a milk crate facsimile of the manger. Sam and I were placed to bracket the kneeling Jesus and Mary, and were directed to look down into the empty milk crate and smile as though we were looking at Jesus. All I could see was the Dairylea cow on the crate silently mooing up at me. The director told us not to worry, Baby Jesus would be in the manger on show night. My heart quickened. The real Baby Jesus? I pictured him asleep in the milk crate, glowing like he did in the stained glass windows in church. I wondered if I would be allowed to hold him.

I mean, if Santa Claus was going around making appearances at the holidays, letting kids sit on his lap in department stores, then I guessed I'd be able to hold the Baby Jesus on my lap in the pageant. I worried that when I met Jesus, he would instantly know that Sam and I weren't really angels and wouldn't like us. I worried that I lacked genuine faith, and unless I truly believed in God, his son might not even show up for our pageant. So I embraced God and began working prayer into my daily life:

"Dear God, thank you for this grilled cheese sandwich which I am about to receive. Amen."

"Oh Lord, let Mommy say Sam can sleep over tonight. Amen."

"Dear Father in heaven, let me win this hand of Go Fish. Amen."

The thing I prayed for the hardest was that God would make Santa Claus bring me a Baby Judy doll for Christmas. Baby Judy was the most beautiful baby doll I had ever seen. I had played with one at rich Emily Green's house. Judy had soft, curly hair and bristle eyelashes that fluttered open when you picked her up from her nap. She had puckered, smiling lips that fit perfectly around the nipple of her baby bottle. When she drank, foamy milk disappeared down her plastic gullet. As Christmas loomed, I doubled my religious fervor, crawling out of bed after lights-out to pray for Baby Judy.

By the time the night of the pageant arrived, I was rabid

with excitement. My family piled into a Checker cab and headed off to the huge, gated fortress on Eighty-ninth Street that was the upper school. Backstage, our mothers dressed us in our angel costumes. Now *that* was heaven. We got soft, flowing white nightgowns cinched with gold drapery cord and silky tassels, glittery angel wings that you put on like a backpack, and headbands with shiny halos attached that seemed to float behind our heads. Our moms kneeled at our feet with safety pins in their mouths, their hands dancing tenderly and efficiently over our bodies as they hemmed and tucked. Then they brushed our ratted, blond hair into silky skeins. Sam and I were transformed from gnawed-up tomboys into graceful seraphs. My father, the man who rolled his eyes at the mere mention of the Lord's name, proudly snapped pictures. Miracles were happening.

The lights went down, and Sam and I stood winged in the wings, our stomachs fluttering, waiting for our cue. We watched enrapt, as the familiar story unfolded on stage. Joseph and Mary wandered into Bethlehem, tired and hungry, and pleading with the innkeeper for a place to stay the night. One of them finally offered his stable and the stage went dark.

A flurry of activity ensued as bales of hay were dragged on and some wooden farm animals were placed upstage. Sam and I shuffled, barefoot, into position in the dark. Shepherds jostled and whispered loudly, nudging each other with their staffs and stepping on each other's sandaled toes. When we had frozen ourselves into position, the lights came up in a white-hot blare.

I took a furtive look around. The stage was crowded with shepherds and angels. Sam and I were the smallest angels—behind us were the "big angels," senior girls with big bosoms and big afros framed neatly by the gold discs of their halos. The choir sang "Silent Night." I saw Sam blinking at me from across the manger. The milk crate was gone and in its place was an old brown cradle, nicked and worn from years of pageantry. I sagged with disappointment. A manger is just a cradle! Just then I realized a holy white light was emanating from within the cradle, and I felt a sudden surge of hope. I leaned in closer to look straight down into the light, certain that I would at last behold the Baby Jesus in all his glory. But when I looked down, it wasn't Baby Jesus in the manger at all—it was Baby Judy.

She was grimy, scuffed, and naked, and she lay suspended over a light bulb by a hammock of rusty chicken wire. Her soft hair had been shaved off, probably to prevent the light bulb from igniting it. Dark, bristly plugs sprouted in rows along her scalp, like a field eaten by locusts. One of her eyes was closed in sweet sleep, while the other was stuck wide open. Her bottle-less lips formed a hungry, yearning "O." I watched as dust motes spiraled slowly through the column of light, coming to settle on Judy's hard, shiny, plastic body. Baby Judy winked up at me. I had never, in all my seven years, seen anything quite so . . . tawdry.

I flushed with anger. So, this was just another adult-world fake out! Another one of those things that isn't what it seems, like the little gingerbread house on the mini-golf course that doesn't open because it has nothing inside. Or giant lollipops in store windows that are really just Styrofoam wrapped with cellophane and ribbon. The world seemed mined with disappointment, and it galled me. I could live with the set pieces and the fake candy, but I wanted the stories to be true. Wasn't the world interesting enough without having to tell a bunch of lies about it? Looking down at Baby Judy in hideous repose over her 100-watt light bulb, I no longer believed in Jesus Christ, or God, or Santa Claus, or fiction of any kind.

I looked up and squinted into the light. It dazzled my wet, salty eyes, blinding me. I felt a strange heat rising beyond it, some presence larger than myself, and all-seeing. It made my heart gallop and filled me with crazy joy. It was the audience. Though I couldn't see them, I knew they were out there, watching me, believing in me.

I suddenly knew that whether or not I believed in God didn't matter; at that moment it was my sacred duty to help tell this story and make the audience believe that Baby Jesus was really in the manger. The only way to do that was to wipe the bitter grimace off my face and start looking angelic.

As I looked out, a fake smile pasted on my face, my eyes slowly adjusted to the light, and faces in the audience began to emerge. I could see my parents beaming up at me from the third row, and my little sister sitting beside them and staring at me with her mouth open. I saw my friends and teachers and all the other people believing in me and I felt my fake smile take hold and grow roots into my heart, warming into something authentic. I had been let in on the big, adult secret: what magic exists in the world is solely of our own making. Our stories are our spells.

I think about telling Franny this story, but decide against it. I won't cast the dogma of atheism over my children. While I pray (well, of course not *literally*) that she doesn't become a Bible-thumping, verse-citing, humorless missionary, I have faith in her to find her own path. Meanwhile, I'll keep preaching the gospel of theater.

Tossing the Cookies

It was coming on Chrismas, and Rae and I had been mulling over the annual problem of teacher gifts. How do we thank the tireless, dedicated individuals who care for our children and demonstrate just how much we value them? More importantly, how do we do it for under ten bucks?

"Cookies!" Rae pronounced over the phone. "We can bake them Christmas cookies!" Rae had come across recipes in a magazine for simple holiday cookies. When Rae makes up her mind about something, it's a done deal.

"Great idea!" I enthused, warming to the idea. "We can put them in gift boxes with tissue paper!" I pictured creamy white boxes tied off with ribbon. "Wait . . ." I was on a roll, ". . . we could even have the kids decorate the boxes with glitter!"

"Yes!" Rae, not usually a chirpy gal, fairly squeaked back at me in glee. It was all coming together. The spirit of the season was upon us.

We convened the next day in my kitchen and stared at

the recipes she had torn from the pages of a women's magazine. The glossy photo of brightly decorated cookies, artfully arranged on a frosted glass Christmas tray, a soft-focus hearth crackling in the background, spoke of comfort and caring, simple pleasures, womanly accomplishment.

We set the kids up at the dining room table with the gift boxes and tubes of glitter glue. Then we tied on our aprons and got to work.

We began with "Dream Bars," which looked like a fairly simple recipe. The ingredients (butterscotch, chocolate chips, shredded coconut, etc.) needed only to be tossed into a Pyrex baking dish, cooked, cooled, and cut into squares.

In less time than it takes to run a bubble bath, we had two dishes of Dream Bars assembled and baking in the oven. On a roll, we proceeded with high spirits to the sugar-cookie dough, which would need some refrigeration before being rolled and cut into festive, seasonal shapes. We happily set to our task, creaming our presoftened butter and mixing in our dry ingredients, feeling like a couple of Ms. Clauses, when . . . oh no, waitaminute—we have baking soda, not baking powder! We weighed the idea of just winging it with the baking soda but then thought better of it. So production ground to a halt as I grabbed my purse and headed out to the supermarket. The express checkout gal was friendly and asked if I was baking.

"Sure am. Christmas cookies!" I said proudly.

"Well . . . good luck," She replied in a doubtful-sounding voice. I wondered what luck had to do with it. Twenty minutes later, I was back just as Rae was pulling the Dream Bars out of the oven. She wore a worried look. "I don't know, can this be right?" she asked, proffering the tray.

I looked down into the pan and was confronted by what looked like a 9" x 12" slab of joke vomit. Pieces of coconut floated in a shining, flesh-colored stew. It was clearly too wet ever to be a bar. "Well, maybe we need to cook it a little more?"

"Yeah?" My friend, usually so confident, so sure of herself, was clearly at a loss.

"Sure, let's put it back in the oven and crank it," I said, faking authority.

We finished the sugar-cookie batter, molded it into logs, and wrapped them in plastic. It felt good putting the wrapped dough in the fridge to harden, like putting money in the bank.

"Damn, we're good!" I proclaimed. That's when we smelled smoke.

"The Dream Bars!" Rae yelped. We yanked them out of the oven to find they had darkened to the color of old scabs. The coconut flakes were singed and smoking.

"They're done," I declared.

"Gee, you think?" deadpanned Rae.

I think it was then we began to realize we were out of our depth. Our training was in liberal arts, not the womanly arts. But we were in too deep to quit, so we trudged on to the grim business of mixing up the Fudgy Nutty Drop Cookies.

When a recipe says "Prep time: 20 minutes," that is assuming you know what you're doing. It also assumes you have bought sweet butter, not salted, and don't have to make yet another trip to the grocery store. The checkout girl greeted me like an old friend.

"Still baking?" she asked sympathetically.

"Yep," was my terse reply.

I returned to find my home in chaos. The kids had lost interest in the gift boxes and Rae was surveying the crafting wreckage strewn out on the dining room table. The kids hadn't exactly drawn designs with the glitter glue. Rather they had simply squeezed great glops of glue onto the tops of the boxes and smeared the puddles with their fingers. Little shining stars floated in a thick mucus of glue that dripped down the sides.

"Pretty," I said.

"Oh yeah, the teachers are gonna *love* these," said Rae.

"All right, let's keep moving. Maybe we can fix this later." I located my double boiler in the way back of a high-up cabinet, and washed the dust off it. Rae broke up the semisweet chocolate chunks. Then I began the backbreaking work of creaming the butter.

As I worked the cold butter with a dinner fork, I mused on my long, expensive, progressive education in which I did not receive a single minute of home economics training. The result is I can write a decent haiku, but I would not be able to wind a bobbin if my life depended on it. I can lambaste the latest Oprah book, but I can baste neither seam nor turkey. It's sad because, in my adult life, I haven't ended up needing to write much haiku. But I sure wish I had enough game in the kitchen to at least pull off some frigging Christmas cookies.

We were somewhere in hour four of our project when we finally got the Fudgy Nutty Drop Cookies into the oven. We wanted desperately to pack it in, but it was time to call the kids in to cut out the sugar cookies.

Our four children came stampeding into the kitchen, half-naked, hands grubby with garden dirt, noses running. After cleaning them up (Prep time: another ten minutes), we set them up with cookie cutters and colored sugar sprinkles.

A frenzy of activity ensued in which the children insisted on cutting the shapes without a care to economizing the dough. So we had to reroll the dough several times, making it softer, warmer, harder to peel off the cutting board. The little men stretched out into oddly misshapen Elephant Men. Heads broke off and were then pressed back onto their bodies. Each one was then sprinkled with a liberal pox of red and green sugar.

The kitchen timer dinged—time to take the Fudgy Nutty Drop Cookies out of the oven! There was a moment of stunned silence between us as we looked at our finished product. My three-year-old, Georgia, pointing a chubby finger at the droppings, was the first to speak:

"Mommy, they look like poops."

And that did it—Rae and I cracked up. We laughed until we were weeping as we looked at our barf bars and our dingleberry drops and our poor, mutant men. We laughed so hard no sound came out of us, other than periodic gasps for air. Something so simple had gone Faustian and nightmarish. We had six batches of Christmas cookies that only Herman Munster would eat.

"We should have just bought them booze," Rae conceded once she had caught her breath. The look of disappointment on the teachers' faces when we gave them the cookie boxes the next day confirmed this, and we swore that next year the gifts will be store-bought.

Reel Baby

The contraction has me pinned to the bed. I am covered in sweat, panting, pushing as hard as I can. "Push!" my midwife yells.

"That's good, honey!" my husband, still crisp in his courtroom pants, encourages me.

I think of my two beloved, already-born daughters, and I grit my teeth and push for all I am worth.

"Cut!" commands Jean, our director. "Good! Let's reset and do another one."

I relax on the bed as the makeup lady swoops in for touch-ups. She spreads another layer of base over my chin zit and glosses my lips. I see myself reflected in her compact. My hair is beautifully disheveled, my skin is dewy with the Evian water they have been misting me with to simulate sweat. If I had looked this good during either of my real-life labors, I might have considered letting my husband bring a camera into the delivery room.

But this is not real life, this is prime-time television. I am here to add my efforts to a long tradition of televised labor and delivery. Honestly, TV birth scenes have always bugged me. The poofy little Lamaze breaths of the "laboring" actress. Pretty, mascara-ed eyes fluttering with imaginary pain. That funny moment when she gets *really, really mad* at her husband and maybe even swears at him a bit. Just adorable. In the televised delivery room the mothers are picture-perfect and nobody shits the bed while birthing babies.

Seven years ago, just as my acting career was heating up, I got pregnant with Franny. I naively thought I would just get all the pregnant roles. Turns out, bona fide pregnant actresses are an insurance risk. After two pregnancies and fifteen pounds of accumulated baby weight, my acting career fell off like an umbilical stump.

I am here because I nailed the labor in the audition. I got the audition because the casting director is a mom at Franny's school. After seven years of rearing and writing, I have landed my big break playing, of all things, a pregnant mom on *The Practice*. In a "ripped from the headlines" plot, my character, Wendy, an eight-months' pregnant Christian Scientist, is on trial for praying while her eldest child died, slowly and painfully, of hantavirus.

My real babies are safely in school and my TV baby hangs on a garment rack in the dressing room. It is a knee-to-shoulder foundation piece with a massive pad sewn onto the front. I strip down to my underpants and glimpse my body in the three-way mirror. As a direct result of Flex Points and hot yoga, I can say I look pretty damn good for a woman who's birthed and nursed a couple of ten-pound babies. I wiggle into the pad and turn back to the mirror. Instantly I am back in my pregnancy body. My belly is a tightly upholstered dome. The cups of my brassiere are heavy as feed bags. I grope my fake breasts, which are firm, pliant, and oddly nubby. I sniff one. I'll be damned—its birdseed. I look back to the mirror. I am the Venus of Willendorf in beige.

The wardrobe mistress enters and has me put on my first costume: a black wool skirt and a blue cashmere sweater set from A Pea in the Pod. My outlook brightens; these are the clothes I jonsed for, but couldn't afford when I was pregnant in real life. The finely tailored separates slide sumptuously over my padded form. I turn to get the side view. In this pregnancy I am carrying all my weight in front. My rear is small and my breasts and belly are picturesquely huge. In the real world I packed my ballooning tush into cheap, badly pilling stretch pants from Target. In this world, I am fashionably fecund. So maybe I won't get to be glamorous in this role, but I will get to have the pregnancy I always dreamed of!

The first few days on set are fun. Not everyone knows I am wearing a pad, which opens up a lot of comic possibilities. At the close of a sober deposition-room scene, I get up from the conference table slamming my swollen abdomen against the edge, making Dylan McDermott gasp. Between setups in the courtroom I do a series of silly walks for the bored extras playing court reporters. I invite strangers to squeeze my soft belly and my birdseed bra so that they too might experience the miracle of television. I hoist my dress in the parking lot to reveal my prodigious rig to Jen, my casting director friend, who is duly impressed. This is the best pregnancy ever! I find that even though people know I'm not really pregnant, I still get the perks: the offered chair, the held door, the special consideration that society reflexively gives a woman with child. Best of all, at the end of the day I go to my trailer and in two minutes, shed all my baby weight without so much as a single sun salutation.

But beneath the many layers of padding, anxiety brews in the pit of my stomach. My TV due date looms. At the end of the week we will shoot the scene in which I give birth. In this way, my TV pregnancy is just like real life—

what is in, must come out, and I have no idea how I will handle the embarrassment of labor, much less the pain. Can I pull it off? As I sit in the courtroom, a hand poised lovingly on my fake belly, I think, *What the fuck am I doing here? On Friday I'll have to throw my legs in the air and fake a vaginal birth in front of all these nice people.* As I sit through multiple takes, listening to Lara Flynn Boyle impugn my Christianity, I find myself Method acting as I pray fervently: *Please, God, please don't let me make a total ass of myself in the birth scene.*

Naturally, this a home birth. My TV home is a softly lit, tastefully Craftsman-esque room with removable walls to accommodate the camera, lights, and crew. Underneath my soft, pricey, never-been-worn Nordstrom nightgown I have on a pair of beige bicycle shorts so no one will have to see my actual vagina as I pretend to squeeze a baby out of it. My thighs have been daubed in peachy body makeup, so that they will be creamy and unmottled for the camera. These are the optimal conditions for a picture-perfect birth.

In fact, this is going to be the birth I always wanted. Instead of my panicky, drug-induced hospital labor, I am going to labor serenely in my own tastefully appointed and unmussed bed. I will be assisted by a kind, holistic midwife, not a cranky shift nurse. There will be no episiotomy, no needles in my spine, no toxic B.O. I look at the childless actress playing my midwife and wonder if she's ever actually witnessed a real birth. If she had, then she'd see how completely ridiculous this whole setup is.

I am suddenly struck by the sheer inanity of this situation—the utter bogosity of it all hits me with the force of a contraction. No! This is wrong! I cannot be complicit in a lie. I cannot allow myself to be lulled by all this loveliness into perpetrating a soft-focus myth. Childbirth is *tough*, people. It is unsightly and seriously painful. It is time to set the record straight on behalf of mothers everywhere. Real women have had their knees to their ears and turned their rectums inside out in order to bring new life into the world. It is my job—nay, it is my *sacred duty*, to inject some hard reality into "must-see TV."

The camera is ready. The assistant director has called for quiet on the set. I lie back down on the bed and prepare myself. I close my eyes and put myself back in my own delivery room, and try to reach for the thing that my subconscious has just about succeeded in blocking out: the pain.

When I think about the pain of labor, I often recall a movie scene. Not a birth scene, but the scene in *Star Wars* when Luke and Princess Leia find themselves dumped out of a Death Star garbage chute and into a giant, intergalactic trash compactor. It's wet, dark, and icky, and something slimy and mysterious is in there with them. Worst of all, the walls are closing in on them fast. The space is getting tighter and tighter and they have no control over it. The walls will squeeze them to death if they don't brace and push themselves out. That is how labor felt to me. Excruciating pain, panic, and doom, laced with deep resolve.

The director calls, "Action!" and I feel the walls closing in, squeezing me harder and harder. I push against them and as I do, a weird little gritty groan, a sound I haven't heard in years, escapes my lips. I push again, harder, and I feel the blood rush to my face, I feel my eyes bulge and real sweat glazing my brow. The pressure builds until I let out a long, gravelly yowl. The director yells, "Cut! Good! Check the gate!" which translated means, that was the one. I fall back onto the bed, panting and exhausted.

Co-actors and grips look at me, stunned. "Are you okay?" they ask, clearly concerned. Nobody figured on this, a woman

turning herself inside out in a birth scene. They were count-
ing on the little pants, the adorable barks of discomfort. They
didn't think they would see my jugular throb or watch me
change color. We're all a little embarrassed.

The next shot is the one where the baby actually comes
out. We rehearse with a facsimile. I lie down and a plastic
baby doll is placed on the bed between my thighs. The midwife pulls it out and holds it up for the camera. Maybe its
the way the light hits the doll's injection-molded curls, but
suddenly I flash back to being seven years old and playing
this very scene with my best friend Gina. In the privacy of
my bedroom we would act out the mystery of birth together, from conception through delivery. I can hear Gina
saying, "Okay, Erika, now it's your turn to be the mommy."
The pretendness of this job hits me—we're all just children
at play here.

Just then the assistant director calls out, "Okay, quiet on
the set—we're bringing in the real baby," and a hush falls
over the sound stage. She is one of triplets, so at five weeks
she is still impossibly small. The nurse lays her down on the
bed at my feet and removes her diaper. The makeup lady
smears her tiny, translucent body with some stuff meant to
look like blood and vernix. The smell wafts up to my nose
and I recognize it as cream cheese and grape jelly. The baby
doesn't like this chilly goop and she begins to cry a thin,
angry wail. Her helpless cry connects to something deep
within my mammalian heart and I want desperately to hold
the baby, to comfort her, to make it okay. The camera rolls
as I reach for her, shaking with raw emotion and smiling
through real tears. I am exhausted, happy, and proud. I
have done it, I have achieved the miracle: I have credibly
given birth on prime-time television.

Volcano

In honor of my thirty-ninth birthday we take the kids to Benihana. In the tiny realm of restaurants that serve food both children and adults will eat, Benihana stands alone. From the onion volcano to the shrimp tossed into the chef's hat, it is a full-on tyke pleaser. They also happen to serve a nice cocktail.

Benihana was something of a tradition in my own family when I was growing up. We marked many birthdays in the Manhattan franchise, and those dinners stand out in my memory as festive times, among some grim family passages. So I bring my own family here on birthdays out of some inchoate urge to make memories.

"I don't feel good," Georgia whines from the back seat of the car, just as we are pulling up to the valet. It's 6:30 and I haven't adequately snacked her in the afternoon. Now she is tired and hungry and heading into a cranky spiral.

"Sweet G, here we are at the restaurant where we'll have a yummy dinner soon. Just hang in there." Her crinkled, angry face looks incongruous with her festive attire: velvety party dress, tights, Mary Janes. She's a regular Surley Temple.

She slumps into the restaurant and our noses are swamped with the smell of frying oil. The air is greasy and heavy.

"It smells bad in here," Georgia says, worry etched into her forehead. Georgia is what my husband calls an "HSP" (highly sensitive person) and has made us leave restaurants because there is some faint, sour note in the air, sometimes detectable only by her.

"It's just the smell of the cooking oil they use. You'll get used to it," I chirp as the maître d' leads us over a small, Japanese footbridge into the main dining room. Being early in the evening, only a few families are there, laughing and talking as their chefs execute acts of derring-do with chicken, steak, or shrimp. They look relaxed and happy, and dammit, this is my birthday—we were going to have fun just like them! We're going to shake off all ill temper and ill health and come together as a loving family around the grill table, reveling in the special feeling that comes with watching your dinner being cooked before your very eyes!

We are seated at a table in the corner, behind a Shoji screen separating us from the bar area. The table is a massive griddle, edged with a ten-inch wooden apron which serves as the dining surface. We immediately order drinks all around, beer for Doug, big sake for Mom, Shirley Temples for Franny and Georgia, the cranky moppet. Waters are poured and salads are brought to the table—small dishes of iceberg lettuce with a spooge of peanut dressing drizzled on top.

"I'm not hungry," Georgia again whimpers.

For some reason I deny her this feeling. I choose to believe instead that she is just so hungry and wrung-out that it has her confused and overemotional. I am convinced that all she needs is a little food to perk her up and get her back in the game. "Just eat a bite of salad," I urge her. My good girl picks at her salad unenthusiastically, her eyes pools of woe.

Franny, sensing that the festive occasion is flagging, does her best to create a total party atmosphere. "Wow! This is so great! I love this restaurant! So Mom, how does it feel to be thirty-nine?"

"Great!" I lie. In fact, in spite of all my efforts, it feels like not much. Thirty-nine is only the year before forty. Its lack of interest underwhelms me. Turning nine at Benihana was so much more fun. I keep having to remind myself why we're here at such expense and discomfort. Oh yeah . . . because tradition dictates that we must make merry around the occasion of our further decay. The drinks come and Doug gamely raises his glass,

"A toast, to Mommy!" Franny hoists her Shirley Temple, her face a banner of good cheer.

"Mommy . . . lappy," Georgia mewls, abandoning her salad and crawling into my lap. Her silky, clean hair blocks out the oily smell of the restaurant, but I know when I kiss her good night later, it will reek of this place.

A young Latino in a tall chef's hat wheels out a cart laden with dishes and knives and parks it beside our table. He swiftly and meticulously sets his stage. Small bowls are lined up in a tight row, each with a different dipping sauce which he has ladled out of a stainless steel vat deftly and precisely. Saran-wrapped plates are uncovered, revealing onions, mushrooms, and bean sprouts. Then he produces a small, white plate which has eight raw shrimp spooning each other in a neat block. With the side of his big knife he delivers them to the cooking surface, where they sizzle and pop. Next the chef picks up a pair of tall salt and pepper shakers and does a drumroll on the edge of the table and then starts flipping them over his shoulders like numchuks, clacking them together theatrically while seasoning our food. In a minute the shrimp has gone from gray to pink and he picks up his big knives and like a culinary Edward Scissorhands, dices the shrimp into tiny bites. In the blur of stainless steel before us, pieces of shrimp fly up into the air, arcing into the top of his tall, white hat. Everyone claps and cheers—everyone except Georgia, who burrows deeper into my bosom.

Next the chef produces a fat slice of onion. Again brandishing his knives, he separates the rings, stacking them in ever-smaller, concentric circles. This is the whole reason we come here: the onion volcano. He pours a bit of oil into the center of the onion and Georgia sits bolt upright in my lap, in what I assume to be excited anticipation of what's next.

Just as the smoke rises from the top of Mt. St. Allium, Georgia convulses. She blows like an overdue volcano, sending a river of vomit lava all over the grill. Chunks of Georgia's digested lunch sizzle on the hot surface, and skitter across it—a revolting entree. The chef is frozen, his knife held aloft as we watch her puke sputter and pop on the grill. Then Georgia erupts again, and this time I'm ready—I point her toward the floor, but instead she vomits all over herself and me. She vomits again, on my shoes, into my purse, and all the time I'm saying, "It's okay, honey, just let it out." I am holding back her hair while she unloads the contents of her stomach onto my lap.

When she is done we are both soaked in a warm, pungent stew of bile. Everyone is frozen, speechless. I look up at the chef, who is quickly putting away his tools. The onion volcano smokes, forgotten at the far end of the table.

"I'm so sorry," I tell him over Georgia's wails, but he is already summoning an unlucky bus boy to clean up the mess. I carry Georgia into the ladies' room to clean her up, but there's only so much you can do with wet paper towels.

I peel off her soggy dress and tights and wrap her in my cardigan, which has miraculously escaped the deluge.

When we come out of the bathroom, Doug has paid for our drinks and gotten our car from the valet. On the ride home, Georgia is her old, chipper self again, but Franny is sober. "I'm sorry your birthday is ruined," she says dolorously.

"Oh sweetheart, it's not ruined at all. This was the most memorable birthday I may ever have. Besides, now we've got a good story to tell, which is really the best gift of all."

"Yeah," says Doug. "Happy Barfday, Mommy." We all laugh long and hard, then go home to order pizza.

Grand Theft Mommy

I was driving through Idlewood and those Ballas mother-fuckers came out of nowhere and shot me down. Now I am dead again and back in purgatory. From the top of these stairs in this quiet park in Jefferson, I can hear the popping of guns far off in the distance. The war rages on at the bottom of these steps, and I just want to stand here, let "C.J."—my virtual alter ego—chill a minute. This is how I discover that if you let your character stand still long enough, he will let an audible fart rip. "Jesus, man!" an old Latino guy mutters at me, "You smell like my ass! You got a pooper problem?"

Sometimes, when my life gets a little too predictable, I go visit the hostile and hilarious world of *Grand Theft Auto: San Andreas*. A place where everyone is looking for a fight, and the only way to win is to murder, steal, fuck, and fight back with abandon. In this world everyone acts on their impulses, nobody watches their language, nobody has to bring a snack. The video game is hated by many (and played by many more) and is currently framing the argument for the need for tighter restrictions on content and ratings in video games as a way to protect America's youth from its immoral influence.

I wish I could say I got *GTA* out of some kind of parental mindfulness—that I was conscientiously monitoring the culture so that I might more effectively protect my children. But in fact, I simply fell for the TV commercial. Choppers swooping and blowing up tanks, a big, black dude with ropy arms clutching an M16, popping off rounds as Guns 'N Roses' "Welcome to the Jungle" screamed in the background. It just looked so cool. I loved the idea of exploring an "open world" and doing anything I wanted. Here in my married, middle-aged, real life, I often feel like I am living in a distinctly closed world—hemmed in by kids, responsibilities, the golden rule. I yearned to blow that shit off and just *roll*. San Andreas seemed as far away as I could get from domestic life while still staying close to home. So my caring husband, ever sensitive to my needs, got me the game for my birthday.

I ripped open the package, thinking I'd load up the disc, pop a beer, and start working my badass shit on the mythical landscape of Los Santos. But I had forgotten my tech handicap. I couldn't even figure out how to turn on my kids' PlayStation. Just figuring out the Gordian knot of cabling and the many input switches and aux buttons that lay in wait behind the components of my entertainment center requires a Y chromosome. I sat, jabbing at the hand controls ineffectually, my voice ramping to a high whine as I called for my husband, not feeling very gangsta'. Who was I kidding?

Finally, I get the game going, but now I'm confronted by the mystery of the controller. There are too many buttons and toggles. I'm told to get on a bicycle and ride, but I just bunny-hop around in place. I finally get going in the right direction and manage to follow Sweet (C.J.'s homie) for two blocks, but it is harrowing. Every time I am about to crash, the controller vibrates in my white-knuckled hands. The stress is intense. In a lame-ass attempt to back up and turn around, I get run over by a truck.

I'm thinking about going down the stairs, stealing a car, and getting back in the game. My boy, Sweet, is pinned down by the Seville Gang and I cannot let him get wasted. As I stand here quietly, the P.O.V. dials in and out. My eyes are a zoom lens on the movie that is C.J.'s life. A tall, saucy babe in a halter dress sashays up the steps toward me and hisses, "You must hate yourself in shoes like that!"

This is how the chicks talk to me in the 'hood. I get no respect because I haven't earned any. I have failed nineteen out of twenty-four mission attempts, I have caused $41,415 in property damage, and have just forty-three bucks in my pocket. I have actually succeeded in blowing up my own car while trying to make a three-point turn. In short, I suck at this game. My sex appeal level is barely readable on the stat bar. I'll never get a 'ho to blow me at this rate.

It's lonely in the 'hood, so I invited my old friend Mark over to play with me. Though he'd never played *GTA* either, Mark has worked in game development and is a font of information.

"This is an FMV, full-motion video," Mark says during the opening movie. We watch as C.J. returns home to a murdered mother and revenge to pay in San Andreas. He hooks up with homies Sweet, Ryder, and Big Smoke, the motion capture animation making the characters eerily real, even as they are rendered in broad, graphic strokes.

GTA isn't so much realistic as it is really cinematic. Many characters are voiced by recognizable stars. There is *mise-en-scène* here, and a steady-cam P.O.V. that zooms and pans over the action. We are not really seeing the world through C.J.'s eyes, but rather we are the camera filming C.J.'s high-impact lifestyle. We are Big Brother, functioning as the ego to C.J.'s twisted id, trying to mitigate the selfish drive that this game demands.

"This is why people aren't going to the movies anymore," Mark enthuses, clearly excited as he jabs at the controls. "This is just as good, if not better, than a film. See, cinema is exterior, and the game is interior. It is you *in* the movie." That is all very interesting, I think, but Mark is hogging the controller. Being a boy, it's like he's magnetically drawn to the thing. Occasionally, he remembers it's my game and my house, and gives it back, but before long it ends up back in his hands.

While Mark drives, I, ever the chick, consult the map and tell him where to go. I am actually happy not to be driving, which is really, really *hard*. The car veers crazily, and I can't control it. But figuring out the map is not so easy, either. For a game this sophisticated, I am surprised at how rough the map is. Points of interest are marked with crude, colored blips. I struggle to get my bearings, but my brain has been shaped by evolution for gathering, not hunting. In real life I navigate with landmarks, using store signs and unusual buildings to mark my way through the world. But the landscape of San Andreas is as flat and repetitive as a Flintstones cartoon background.

Mark is hell-bent on accomplishing missions. "All right, let's tag up some turf!" I, on the other hand, want to get C.J. something to eat, some rest, maybe some pussy. I would be happy just to wander around the streets of Los Santos on foot, poking into stores, getting tattoos, shooting hoops, changing my 'fro at the barbershop. In fact, I find myself longing to play a game that would draw on my nurturing skills, one I might be able to win. Something that involves carpooling and sandwich-making. But if I want to get ahead in this game, it would behoove me to pick up a shovel and smash somebody's face in.

"What's so interesting about this game," Mark observes while kicking the shit out of an innocent bystander to reap the five bucks in her purse, "is it forces you to behave in a socially unacceptable manner. You cannot play without committing serious crimes." I'm starting to wonder if I'm too girly to ever be good at this. I've got enough testosterone to want to play the game, but maybe not enough to win.

Much has been made of the violence in *GTA*, but the violence is merely the means to an end of accomplishing missions. What surprises me about *Grand Theft Auto* is not its brutality, which I was fully expecting, but its humor. The game, designed by Scotsmen, is one long spoof on American culture, complete with prattling talk radio and ads that skewer American consumerism, like the commercial for the fictional De Koch Fine Jewelers: *"Shut that bitch up with ice."* An irony of the current hoopla around GTA is that it is being blamed for our cultural downfall, when really it's just throwing our own culture back in our faces. It is an homage to the worst and the best of America, from drive-by shootings to Patsy Cline.

One of the great pleasures of the game is listening to San Andreas radio, where every station from reggae to country to '90s hip-hop is jamming and mostly old school. Cruising down a boulevard in a stolen lowrider convertible, with an orange sun melting into the horizon, listening to Ice Cube's "It Was a Good Day," is as chill as it gets. It makes me glad to be a part of this cultural mess we're in.

Every generation spawns some new cultural artifact that transfixes teens and horrifies adults: comic books, rock 'n' roll, punk, rap. I was curious, now that I am finally a parent and no longer the rebellious teen, to find out whether this game would disturb me as much as the Sex Pistols disturbed my own parents. It certainly gets Hillary Clinton's dander up—she has come out strongly for tighter regulations on gaming access and content. But instead of outrage I feel reassured that the things I have always loved about pop culture—play, invention, humor, and a healthy disregard for boundaries of taste—are alive and well—at least in *Grand Theft Auto*.

Mark, being a responsible grown-up, has obligations that prevent him from hanging out with me all day playing *GTA*. He goes home to his family and leaves me alone with the game. I try to make sense of it, but keep getting lost, killed, or yelled at by my pissed-off homies. I feel like I could be good at this if I could only read the map or drive a car. I die one grisly death after another: gunshot, car crash, car fire, you name it. And always I end up back at the top of the steps in Jefferson.

Mark sends me to his friend Gus for a game tutorial. When I get to Gus's house, he hands me a cold beer and the controller. A connoisseur of pop culture, his entertainment console includes a PS2, Game Cube, XBox, and an old Dreamcast unit. Gus looks old enough to be my kid brother, and despite a lifetime spent watching movies and playing violent video games, he is a gracious and intelligent man. He kindly doesn't laugh at me as I total my car trying to get out of C.J.'s *cul de sac,* though Sweet, ever the bitch, yells at me from the screen, "C.J., you *asshole!*"

Gus tries to get me to relax. "Just drive around and don't worry about getting anywhere." I try to keep an even touch on the button that accelerates the car, but I've got a lead finger. My car lurches and jerks forward. When I take out a gaggle of pedestrians, he observes, "You're not really a gamer, so you don't have all the built-in training. The language of driving a car in a game isn't ingrained."

"You can say that again," I reply, straining to keep my car from going off a bridge. "I used to play as a kid. I liked *Pac-Man* and *Galaga*."

"Those were good games," Gus says of those '80s arcade games. "Anyone could play them. There was a time when a bunch of people who played games stopped (when the game industry crashed in the mid '80s) and they missed the learning curve of how to play these complex games." This describes me perfectly. I was a *Ms. Pac-Man* champ through college, then got distracted by real-life games, like earning a living and finding a decent boyfriend. As a result, I never got a firm grip on joysticks.

Pac-Man is to *Grand Theft Auto* what tic-tac-toe is to chess. The rules of today's games are confusing and revealed slowly. It is a vastly complex world. It's not about learning how to win the game, but learning how to be in the game. In his book, *Everything Bad is Good for You*, Steven Johnson argues these games are making us smarter. "The great secret of today's video games . . . is how difficult the games have become," he wrote in an *L.A. Times* op-ed piece. "That difficulty is not merely a question of hand-eye coordination; most of today's games force kids to learn complex rule systems, master challenging new interfaces, follow dozens of shifting variables in real time, and prioritize between multiple objectives." In *GTA: San Andreas,* a simple dance party on the beach has me rhythmically hitting buttons in a random pattern to make C.J. boogie. I can feel my poor, aging brain straining to refresh dilapidated neural pathways in order to accommodate all this new information. This is not a pastime for the intellectually inert.

Gus gets me through the "Nines and AK's" mission. Then we buy some "colors" at the Binco store, work out at the gym, get some hot wings at the Cluckin' Bell. By the end of the night I see how the game works, but I doubt I'll ever possess the confidence and fluidity of play that Gus has.

Driving home from Gus's house, I feel for the first time the visceral influence of the game. Navigating traffic post-*GTA* is an altered experience. I feel as reckless and invincible as a teenager with a beer buzz. Cruising down Western, a car in front of me suddenly changes lanes to reveal a homeless man wandering across the road. His face, illuminated by my headlights, is etched in animated madness. He is muttering to himself, probably saying something *GTA*-ish like, *"I like sexy cartoons!"* For a moment, I consider running him over, but stop myself. He probably doesn't have any cash or weapons.

If you play *GTA* in Los Angeles, there is a surreal feeling of crossover. After all, "San Andreas" is a stand-in for California, and the city of "Los Santos" is recognizable as L.A. It is both strangely familiar and completely foreign. I know it, but I don't know my way around it. In real life, I live on the edge of the 'hood. Gang tags appear on our garage door overnight, cars get stolen, homes are robbed. Ghetto Birds fly over our house most nights, their high beams probing our backyard for perps like C.J. Playing the game gives me a strange new perspective on some of my shady neighbors. I feel something akin to empathy. They are just trying to survive, get some health points. Who am I to judge them?

I don't deny that playing this game can affect your real-world behavior, but in a socialized adult, that effect is momentary. By the time I get back home from Gus's, I am grounded in my own reality once again. But what about the game's influence on the impressionable minds of children?

I don't live in fear of video games. Maybe that's because I have girls, who would much rather play with their hamsters and build fairy houses in the backyard than go on simulated killing sprees. My friend Judie, however, is in constant negotiation with her ten-year-old son Alex over his access to his Game Boy, and is currently debating whether he can have an XBox for his birthday. These limitations haven't quelled his enthusiasm. My daughter tells Alex I am playing *Grand Theft Auto,* and my stock with him instantly rises. He gives me tips and cheats for a game he's never played and won't be allowed to play for another eleven years.

"Here's how you spawn a rhino tank," Alex says from the swimming pool, where he is in the middle of a lesson with my kids, shouting out the secret button combination: "Circle, circle, L1, circle, circle, L1, L2, R1, triangle, circle, triangle." He gets the cheats off the G4 Web site, mentally cataloguing them for the day when he will actually get to play.

"Okay, Alex," his mother frowns, "pay attention to the lesson." He reluctantly goes back to his breaststroke.

"Look, your health is down. Let's go find a soda machine," says Jake, without taking his eyes off the screen. He expertly steers C.J.'s car off a freeway exit, precisely locating a soda machine. "Did you know if you drink a soda you get full health?" Then he adds, "I quit drinking soda about six months ago."

Jake is a clear-eyed boy of twelve. He gets a cold one for C.J. and, sure enough, as C.J. guzzles, his red health meter goes to full. It's just another little Rockstar joke. This is the fun of a topsy-turvy world. What's bad is good and vice versa.

Jake and I are in his family's rec room, surrounded by

the artifacts of his enriched upbringing: books, videos, puzzles, tubs of sports equipment. I am folded into a kid-sized butterfly chair, watching him play. He tells me he's not that good, but Jake's got C.J. out the door and over to Colonel Fuhrburger's house inside of a few minutes and is executing a seamless home invasion that I have failed four times already. There is a certain careless freedom in Jake's movements through the virtual world. The controller is an extension of his body. Whereas I wince and hesitate my way down the street, Jake bangs the truck along, hugging turns, pedal to the metal. He ditches the truck and steals a motorcycle to perform a stunt jump on the freeway. The bike pinwheels through the air and lands thirty feet below, shiny side up, scoring us major points.

Next, Jake takes me on the "Robbing Uncle Sam" mission, and we drive down to the National Guard Depot by the Ocean Docks. He expertly shoots out the switch, opening the warehouse door where crates of ammo are stored. Simultaneously loading crates into his van with a forklift and shooting National Guardsmen, Jake explains why he doesn't play video games much.

"There's too much else to do. If I play by myself it's because I'm bored and that doesn't happen that often." He knows kids who are hardcore gamers. "They're freaky. They don't have much patience. It's like they don't have much of a life. You can't make many friends when you're playing a video game." This is my biggest problem with *Grand Theft Auto*: It is a single-player game, and as such, kind of lonely. Jake would rather be outside hitting tennis balls with his dad, which, after an hour of playing with me, is exactly what he goes and does.

I am alone again at the top of the steps in Jefferson. The early morning gray saturates with color as the sun rises on another day in San Andreas. I know I am not long for this world. I came too late and with too many obligations to linger. But I'm glad I got this far. Now I know that the video games are not destroying our youth's moral fiber. It's more the fact that kids are stuck inside playing in the virtual streets because the streets they live on are too dangerous. And yes, I do worry about angry, isolated kids playing *Grand Theft Auto* all day, because no one is there to toss them a ball or nag them to do something else. Some of those kids may turn into sociopaths because of their exposure to little else than simulated violence. But you've got to wonder: Is this the fault of a game or of poor parenting and by extension a society that pays lip service to "family values" but does precious little to support them? That Hillary Clinton and her ilk are trying to score their own political health points with this ass-backward logic makes me seethe with anger. I take off down the steps in Jefferson one more time, looking for someone to take it out on.

Cereal Killers

They strike in the morning. Padding silently in bare feet, voices quiet with sleep. They stand in the doorway of the pantry, choosing their next victim. Will it be Rice Krispies or Smart Start, Frosted Mini Wheats or Honey Nut Cheerios? They scan the boxes, checking for free prizes and special offers, but finally, as always, they are inevitably, instinctually drawn to the brand with the highest sugar content. Should there be a box of Lucky Charms alone in a group of high-fiber, low-sugar cereals, then they will both pounce on it, devouring it until it is gone and they are licking the pastel, vitamin-fortified dust off their sticky fingers.

They work quickly and quietly. All I can hear from my bedroom is their spoons clinking against their bowls, the slurp of milk. Soon they will be sated and will move on to morning cartoons, their voices spiking with their blood sugar.

As I listen to them I start thinking about what cereal I am going to be having this morning. Wheat Chex? Grape Nuts? Honey Bunches of Oats (with Almonds!)? It is a question I have relished every single morning of my life. My young have inherited their hunger for dry cereals from me. I enacted this same scene with my younger sister (who, with her children, now strikes terror into the hearts of Cleveland-area cereals), sitting at the table, slurping up great spoonfuls of Kaboom or King Vitamin in silence, reading the backs of the boxes over and over again as though they held clues to our future.

Of course, the boxes were much better back then. There was real information, games to be played, actual prizes to be had inside. Bright, colorful toys a child could choke on. Now it's all mail in prizes and rebates, which goes against the whole point of cold cereal: instant fucking gratification.

Cereal is for people who like to live in the moment. It is quick to prepare, requires no planning, must be eaten immediately before it grows soggy, satisfies instantly. There are few foods (or experiences) in life as gratifying as cereal.

We are breakfast people. Our family revels in the morning meal. When my daughters are grown, what they will probably remember most is breakfast. Our routine is simple and predictable: six days a week we all eat cereal, then on one weekend day, when we are at leisure, we celebrate with waffles or pancakes. My husband and I have been dubbed by our children "The Pancake Lady" and "The Waffle Man" for our breakfast specialties. On Saturday or Sunday mornings, after the kids have committed granicide and are hopped up on a couple of hours of Sponge Bob, they will wake whichever one of us who can best satisfy their renewed appetites.

In most households, a waffle marks a special occasion. It is the breakfast that says, "Merry Christmas!" or "Congratulations on Your Report Card!" In our home that role falls to the Dutch Baby. The Dutch Baby is of unknown origin (it is almost certainly not Dutch). The recipe comes from a page out of Doug's grandmother's cookbook. Mama Grace, a sensible, thrifty woman of the heartland, had a weakness for baked goods. Doug suffered a chubby childhood under her tutelage. She plied him with maple bars, lemon squares, and chicken-fried steaks, and only after he grew to adulthood and escaped his heavily matriarchal boyhood home was he able to slim down into foxy manhood.

Mama Grace sadly passed before I came on the scene, but her most lasting legacy is the Dutch Baby, which features flour, a dozen eggs, and about four sticks of butter. The melted mixture is poured into a shallow baking dish and put into a hot oven where the mixture inflates, the corners magically rising up into curled points (like wooden shoes!) while the middle stays flat and moist. The final product—golden brown, flaky on the edges, and slightly chewy in the middle—is best served with powdered sugar, syrup, and a mélange of fruits (we favor apples, pears, and bananas). It is a Cereal Killer's Holiday. It resets our appetites for the following weekday's sprinkle and splash.

It's not that our family doesn't enjoy scrambled eggs and toast, sausage and omelets, the occasional hash brown or bowl of oatmeal. It's just that we consider those foods more appropriate for dinner. We prefer empty carbs and sugar in the morning. In fact, we relish the mid-morning sugar crash. I have passed my hypoglycemia on to my children, and at about 10:30 in the morning we become hazy and unfocused, moody and depressed. Doug, expert in recognizing the signs, immediately administers nuts and cheeses and slices of turkey so we can make it to lunch. A sugary breakfast just makes lunch so much batter. I mean, better.

So if you are a puffed and/or sugar-coated grain, then beware: you will not survive long in our house. For we will hunt you down and kill you. We will savagely rip open your box and tear at your plastic liner, sending your sweet nuggets skittering across cold linoleum. We will shake you into a shallow bowl and cover you with milk. We will attack you with shiny spoons, heedless of your cries of Snap, Crackle, or Pop. Milk will be spilled in our savage feast. Then, what's left of you will be hastily rewrapped and stuffed onto our pantry shelves, where we keep our other half-eaten victims. You will wait there in the dark, for our next attack, which can often happen late at night. For it is then, before retiring, that I personally often need one more taste. Just a small bowl to get me through the night, to quell the ever-present hunger, to taste your sweet clusters on my tongue, the beguiling crunch of your almonds, the slightly soggy flake of your flesh.

Your picture may end up on the very milk carton that sits beside our next victim at the breakfast table tomorrow morning.

Franny and Zoo

It's a hot, nutty day at the zoo. Spring-break crowds stand five-deep at the railings of the cages, ogling the animals. The animals ogle us back—after nearly a week of solid rain, everyone is happy to be outside. All the critters are stirred up, agitated, ranging around on either side of the bars.

We are a group of four women chaperoning twelve children, ranging in ages three to fourteen. It takes commando-like skills to keep this operation togther, and we vigilantly track children as they dart excitedly around the exhibits. To complicate matters, we've rented two covered, double strollers, and the kids switch out of them so many times, one never knows who's riding and who's run off ahead. Through a complex system of head counts and hand-offs, barked orders, and the occasional cell-phone call, we four moms have the day in hand.

Our first clue that spring fever had struck the zoo is at the reptile house. Usually the glass-fronted exhibits are little more than a series of reptillian tableaux, but today there is a frenzy of activity. Snakes coil into elaborate knots and lizards leap. At the turtle terrarium our group grinds to a halt to watch the novel sight of two tortoises humping in slow motion.

"What are they doing?" Georgia, my four-year-old, asks, her question hanging in the air as we moms look at each other, groping for the right spin for the truth.

"They're playing leap frog!" Franny answers. Everybody laughs and our group moves on.

Though I love my children equally, there are days when I enjoy one more than the other. Today Franny's stock is high. While Georgia grumbles and stays in the stroller, complaining of heat and hunger, Franny flits cheerfully to each exhibit, carefully reading the signs, making thoughtful observations and drawing measured conclusions. She is wearing her black Powerpuff Girl baseball cap and has pulled her ponytail out the back of it. My heart spasms with love as I contemplate that ponytail.

After a couple of hours our group is overcome by full bladders and empty stomachs as we arrive at the monkey habitat. We stake out a bench and Teresa goes for snacks while Kimberly takes whoever needs to pee to the bathroom. I stay behind with the rest of the kids to watch the monkeys.

The apes, like the reptiles, are restive. They are mounting each other and swapping partners like a bunch of swingers at Plato's Retreat. The behavior is blatantly sexual and it becomes my job to explain the birds and the bees and the monkeys in the trees to the startled children.

"Are they hurting each other?" Franny asks, her gray-green eyes searching my expression.

"No, sweetie, they aren't hurting each other."

"Then what are they doing?"

I have explained sex to Franny, but there are younger children here, children that don't belong to me. Not sure if

I am authorized to dispense the truth, I hedge, "They are playing."

Teresa returns, bearing hot dogs and french fries. Together we explain to the children that what they are doing feels good in spite of appearances, and that it will result in more monkeys. The children silently pump fries into their mouths as they watch a simian couple frantically hump while swinging off a large, knotted length of rope. Teresa leans in and says under her breath, "This is getting *me* hot." Her cell phone rings and it is Kimberly, who is at the lion habitat with her kids. "We'll be right over!" Teresa hangs up. "Kim says the lions are getting it on, too!" We break camp and head over to check it out.

By the time we get there the female is tired of tussling and lies supine under a scruffy tree. She is clearly wanting to take a postcoital nap, but the male isn't done with her. He pounces on her and bats at her, like a naughty kitten, his tail twitching with come-hither mischief. Franny has seen enough today to know the score. "He's too frisky to hear her limits."

The day is winding down and our group is completely tapped from the chaos and energy all around us. We head toward the zoo's exit, stopping at the stroller kiosk to return our rentals. I bend down to tie Georgia's shoe and think, *Where's Franny?* But my internal, automated surveillance system answers, *She's with the other kids, getting ice cream.* I tighten the laces on Georgia's other shoe for good measure.

I am smelling the barn, relaxing, anticipating a cold beer at home, satisfied in my super-momness. But dammit, where's Franny? Giving Georgia's shoelace a final yank, I stand up and look over to the ice cream cart, scanning the heads around it. I wait patiently for her blond ponytail under her black cap to bob into view. But it doesn't.

Some mothers, at this point, might start to panic. But I don't. I have a long lag time on fear. Not many bad things happen in my world, least of all on sunny, perfect days like this. I take Georgia by the hand and lead her over to the table where the other kids are sitting, having a final ice cream binge.

"Hey guys, where's Franny?" I ask. Faces wreathed in chocolate turn to me with blank expressions. "Dani, wasn't she with you?"

"Nuh-uh," Dani replies, spooning beads of freeze-dried ice cream into her gap-toothed mouth. T.J., the eldest at fourteen and our stand-in adult, looks at me mystified. "I thought she was with you." A hairline fracture of fear appears in my heart.

"T.J., stay here with the kids," I command as I drag Georgia back to the stroller return to find the other moms. Kim and Teresa are walking toward me, and I guess my face must have communicated the problem.

"What's up?" Kim asks.

"Franny. Where's Franny?" I beseech her.

Immediately the women start calling her name. We circulate the area. Franny knows the rules; if I call her name, she must answer immediately. Usually when I call her name she magically appears, crawling out from under garment racks or jumping out of doorways. I listen for her sweet voice to answer back, "Here I am, Mama!" But all I hear is the rumbling of the crowd around me. We are near the exit, and a sea of people are heading out into the parking lot. The entrance/exit to the zoo is under construction. The turnstiles have been removed and a wooden facade apologizing for their dust funnels visitors on a long, unsupervised walkway toward the parking lot. It would be so easy to walk out with someone else's child. My heart starts jumping around, beating at the bars of my ribcage.

"Franny! Franny!" My voice is tight with fear.

"Mommy, I'm scared." I look down and see Georgia, still attached to my hand. I pick her up and sling her onto my hip.

"It's okay, Georgie, we'll find her."

By now everyone in the area is aware a child is missing. A young man in a Lakers hat asks what she was wearing. I stop and try to conjure an image of my child's outfit.

"A black Powerpuff hat, and . . ." I stand there, mute, mumbling, ineffectual.

My friend Kimberly, a fierce and fearless black woman with a voice that can wake the dead, is completely on the case. Her first order of business is to barrel into the men's restroom to see if Franny's being held inside. I see surprised gentlemen exiting the bathroom, zipping their flies.

I rush back to the kids' ice cream table and deposit Georgia with T.J.

"Dani," I ask Franny's best friend, "what was Franny wearing today?"

"Her kitty t-shirt and blue flowered pants," she replies without skipping a beat. Girls.

I go back to look for the Lakers guy who asked me what she was wearing, but he's gone. I look around for him for a minute before I realize I am looking for the wrong person. I should be looking for my daughter. I prowl through the crowd, a knot of instinct and fear. I need to see my child, to smell her and tuck her back into my pouch.

I run to the gift shop, remembering she had brought her allowance and had been hoping to spend it. "Franny! Franny!!" I yell, trying to jolt customers out of their shopping dazes, but they just stand and stare, like lizards behind glass.

I run back to my friends, who are now giving my daughter's description to zoo security. It has come to this. I hear

her sweet name crackle over their walkie-talkies. My mouth
is dry.

The day has gone from wild to insane. In this place
where animals fuck and fight, my daughter has gone missing. I stare out toward the parking lot, an unregulated veldt
of slamming car doors, engines starting up, and windowless
vans pulling out, heading toward the freeway. If someone
has taken Franny out there, then chances are I won't ever
see her again. This possibility rakes over me, making me
sick to my stomach. I am caught between horror and disbe-
lief. I start to howl. A long, pained yowl of fear spirals up
out of my gut. People stare and skirt around me.

I wander down the long gangway toward the parking
lot, still barking her name. I realize that I am incapable of
doing anything useful or effectual. Why in this time of crisis
have I shut down? Then I see Teresa running toward me.
She is waving her arms at me and shouting something. As
she gets closer I hear her words, "We found her!"

She takes me by the hand and pulls me down, down the
gangway, almost to the parking lot. I turn the corner and
see my girl, baseball cap and all, walking toward me with a
security guard by her side, looking calm and happy.

And what do I do? I yell at her, "No, no, no, no, no, no,
no! Where the hell were you!" The fear in my face and
voice cause her to tremble. I am scaring her. Good.

Franny's eyes are wide and shining with tears. "Momma,
I thought you were still behind me. I just kept walking. I
didn't know!"

"But I wasn't with you!" I shouted, my fingers digging
into her soft arms.

"I know. When I realized I was lost I found a lady with
kids just like you told me." I have taught my daughters, in
the event they should get lost, to seek out a mom with kids

or a teenage girl to help them. I don't want them trusting some weird rent-a-cop. "I did the right thing!"

She has. I look at my precious young, and suddenly understand that on some level, I have fulfilled my evolutionary purpose. Here is my child—a reasoning, resourceful, and responsible person who can make it in the jungle. I fall to my knees in front of her and gather her to my chest, nuzzling my face into her neck, resisting the urge to lick her. The beast inside me quiets and retreats back into its lair. "You did exactly right, Franny," I say, tucking her under my wing. "Let's go home."

Zorba the Geek

One of the greatest gifts my mother gave us as kids was free access to the record player. As long as it wasn't "the grown-up hour," that time of each day when my parents used the living room exclusively for cocktails and conversation, the phonograph and living room belonged to us. My sister and I spent countless hours spinning records and dancing ourselves into a froth. Our parents had a solid record collection that featured not only the requisite Nilsson, Beatles, and Blood, Sweat, and Tears albums of the day, but also a great many film soundtracks. I can remember an entire month I spent hurling myself off the couch and across the shag to the soaring zither of "Zorba the Greek." I also remember performing an emotive, interpretive dance to Johnny Mercer's stirring *Darling Lili* score. My mother was always a willing and appreciative audience.

Now I am a mother of two passionate living-room dancers. Every day of the week there is some kind of a dance party going on in our house.

Home dancing is a strange and glorious beast. Club

dancing must be cool, but at home a girl can take risks. Whether it's attempting a split, spinning dizzily in a twirly skirt, or just knotting your t-shirt under your braless boobs and ponying to Madonna, *at Club de su Casa* your inner Dancing Queen is free to boogie down.

As a mother, I am proud to say I have provided my children with all they need to nurture their own nascent Dancing Queens: a spacious living room, secondhand furniture to jump on, and free access to the stereo and a variety of CDs.

At our club the DJ is usually Georgia. At three years old she could work the hi-fi like a pro, changing CDs smoothly and quickly. She rarely takes requests and her taste is decidedly eclectic. Georgie's play list features Cher, Los Lobos, *The Wizard of Oz* soundtrack, The Bar-Kays' "Soul Finger," the music of Raymond Scott, and the godforsaken, corporate-brainwash CD that they hand out to children in the Build-A-Bear store. This is the price you pay for a no-limits policy with kids and music: sometimes you end up listening to lyrics like, *"Choose me, stitch me, fill me up. Fluff me, dress me, fill me with love."* But then, the other day, Georgia performed for me a trembling, tender ballet solo to "Teddy Bear Dance" that brought tears to my eyes. So I stand by my policy.

I bought my kids a boxed set of disco tunes recently so that I might introduce them to the hits of my day. You see, a mother's work is so much about passing on the culture's rich traditions to her young. I thought Franny would enjoy enacting the pathos of "Billy, Don't be a Hero" just as I did. I love watching kids' literal interpretations of lyrics, making a muscle on "Hero" and ducking down on "Billy keep your head low-ow-ow." Show tunes are, of course, the manna of the living-room dancer. I can still remember some of the explosive jazz-hands moves I did to Judy Garland's "Get Happy" or the slapstick free-for-all inevitably inspired by "Make 'Em Laugh."

There was a time, before I had children, when I wore black eyeliner and miniskirts and haunted the nightclubs of New York City. I couldn't imagine the drab lives of the poor suckers who stayed at home with kids. Now, as I kick off my slippers and gyrate in sweats beside my ecstatic off-spring, cutting our living room rug, I feel like I finally made it into the hottest club in town.

When Night Was Falling

Franny loves an audience. Whenever a group of adults is assembled, she, in the manner of precocious children everywhere, wants to put on a show. At the moment she is obsessed with *Wicked,* the Broadway musical about the college friendship between Glinda and the Wicked Witch of the West. Her favorite song is "Popular" and she has performed it (along with her own kicky choreography) for every adult we know. She is so my daughter.

I was a musical-obsessed kid in the winter of 1975 when my family made our annual trip from our home in New York to Los Angeles to visit my mother's parents. Designed by my granddaddy in the '50s, their house was a sleek, Neutra-inspired affair perched on a Pacific Palisades hillside, offering a sweeping ocean view that an eleven-year-old couldn't have cared less about.

But the house itself was the ideal setting for a girl living in her own MGM musical—all glass doors, white floors, stylishly decorated by my Grandma Dorothy. A palm tree grew out of the living room floor and crystals splashed rainbows across the walls. I'd slide across the slick, terrazzo floors in sock feet like Gene Kelly in *An American in Paris* or clickety-tap on them in my Mary Janes like Fred Astaire. I could tinkle the keys on the white baby grand, or bob like a Ziegfeld Girl in the sunken bathtub, surrounded by jungle fronds, lathering up with richly scented, seashell-shaped soaps. I spent hours in the swimming pool, smiling underwater like Esther Williams, and lounged in "the chatter pit," a subjacent, shag-lined den that had a TV with a *remote control.* I sprawled on the long banquette sofa, like Jeannie in her bottle, blinking my way through channels, searching for my favorite TV shows on the unfamiliar West Coast stations.

On this particular trip, my grandparents threw one of their big parties. I helped prep, buffing their colored Lucite coffee table knickknacks, Windexing the huge, sliding glass doors, lighting and launching floating candles onto the pool. Their guests were a mix of comedy writers and tennis partners, all of whom seemed incredibly old, smoky, and uninterested in me. Forgotten by the grown-ups, I stayed up way past my bedtime, gorging on Spanish peanuts, lulled by the drone of adult conversation. It was late in the evening when my mother found me out by the pool, woozy from Shirley Temples.

"There's someone inside I want you to meet," she said.

"Who?"

"His name is Johnny Mercer. He's an old friend. You've met him once before, but you probably won't remember him."

"Mommy . . ." I whined, not wanting to give up my warm, sleepy spot by the lava brazier.

"He wrote the lyrics for a lot of famous movie songs."

"Really, like what?"

"*Seven Brides for Seven Brothers, Breakfast at Tiffany's, Darling Lili.*"

I was suddenly wide awake. I loved all those movies, but *Darling Lili* was my current obsession. Though I had never seen the movie, I had spent that fall memorizing the soundtrack album.

Mercer was alone in my grandaddy's study. This room was different from the others. It wasn't like a movie set, it was a real place where actual work happened. The walls were hung with photos and memorabilia from a lifetime spent writing for radio, sitcoms, movies, and magazines. There were awards, autographed posters, and framed Playbills. Stacks of scripts surrounded his typewriter. The room was dim and had the sweet, pungent smell of pipe smoke mixed with chlorine. Mr. Mercer, sitting on a low sofa, looked like an ordinary old man. I had half hoped he'd be wearing a top hat and tails, but he was in slacks and a sports coat. He had a kind smile and seemed tired. He greeted me warmly and asked me the usual kid questions— how old was I, how did I like school, was I having a fun trip? Then he said, "Your mother tells me you're a fan of my songs."

"Did you really write *Darling Lili*?"

"Well, I wrote the lyrics. Do you have a favorite song?"

"'The Girl in No Man's Land.'"

"*Really!*" He seemed surprised and interested. I sensed I had an audience, a thing I was always on the lookout for.

"I can sing it for you if you'd like."

Mercer laughed, then looked me in the eye. "Would you? That would be lovely."

Suddenly my whole body got hot and clammy as I realized what I'd gotten myself into. I straightened up and started singing in a soft, wobbly voice.

I knew I could sing this song better. I closed my eyes and pretended I was back in my living room in New York.

I picked up steam and as so often happened, I became

taken by the sound of my own voice. I fancied I sang it just like Julie Andrews did on the album. I opened my eyes to see a look of utter shock on Mercer's face. I faltered and stammered. I had no idea what the next lyric was.

". . . *Cold and lonely* . . ." Mercer fed me the line and the rest of the song came rushing back.

I finished and Mr. Mercer applauded me. My mother draped her arm around my shoulder and I noticed that Granddaddy had slipped into the room. He stared at me from under bushy eyebrows as though he were seeing me for the first time. I assumed these grown-ups were all stunned by my exquisite voice, but now, thirty years later, I think it may simply have been the incongruity of an eleven-year-old girl singing a ballad about a hooker.

Mr. Mercer thanked me and I left him. A month later I received a package of *Darling Lili* production stills and a note from him, thanking me again for my song. He died the following year. It wasn't until much later that I truly realized who I had serenaded in my grandfather's study, and how many songs Mercer had written that I love to this day. Only now can I appreciate that a child memorizing his songs may have meant a lot to a man whose life, and work, was nearly over.

The house Granddaddy designed is still up on Tellem Drive. I drove out there with Franny the other day on a whim and knocked on the door. It is owned now by a distinguished German film actor, and his son graciously gave me a tour. The master bath has been remodeled, but the rest of the house is just as I remember it, if a little smaller and dingier. I took a picture of Franny standing by the pool brazier, now the age I was then, and thought about the people who had gathered there to drink, laugh, and tell their stories of young Hollywood—a place and time that has long since faded into black and white.

Operation Peaceful Summer

Out on the drill floor of the Army Reserve Building everything is in chaos. Kids are running around, shooting bas-
kets, doing gymnastics, working on hip-hop dance routines.
In an odd twist of municipal fate, the City of Culver City,
which owns this building, has seen fit to rent out the space
not being used by the National Guard (as they have all
shipped off to Iraq) to Camp Planet Janet.

The camp is named for its director, Janet Horn, a tall,
buxom woman with a salt-and-pepper crew cut and an
easy, welcoming manner. My kids have been coming to
Planet Janet for years. In addition to swimming, dancing,
and arts and crafts, Planet Janet offers a strong "Victory
Over Violence" program—essentially basic training in conflict resolution and peace activism. Each week, campers ex-
plore a different global region and its culture, then put on
plays depicting the enslavement of native peoples by imperi-
alists, or the peaceful resolution of differences through dialogue. My kids like it because you get to do pretty much
whatever you want here, and after a year of public-school

drills, it's nice to be able to just sit around and make cootie catchers all day.

The Army's recruiting table is set up by the front door. At the beginning of the summer it was orderly, with displays of pamphlets neatly arrayed between two three-sided, man-sized, cardboard pillars. One face of the column shows a clean-cut guy in khakis with the word "Citizen" emblazoned alongside. Turn the column and you see the same guy in full uniform with the caption "Soldier." The "Soldiers" have been turned to face the wall, the recruiting pamphlets are gone, and the table is heaped with kids' towels, dirty socks, and water bottles. It has now become the lost and found.

Supply Sergeant Alberto Rivera is literally holding down the fort. With all of his comrades off fighting the newly launched war in Iraq, it is his job to keep the base operations running smoothly. But with one hundred screaming kids outside his office door and no backup, he is clearly outnumbered. I wander into his office to have a look around. I am intrigued by this quiet, orderly, military man surrounded by frantic peaceniks and want to know how he's doing.

I tap at the door jamb and he looks up. "May I come in?"

"Affirmative," he replies. I can't believe he just said that. Nobody I know has ever used that word unless they were joking. I introduce myself to him as a camp mom and my affect borders on the obsequious. I want him to know that despite our obvious differences, I am friend, not foe. He is polite and welcoming and invites me to look around.

His office is a big supply closet with a desk at one end. Flak jackets hang in rows from the ceiling. Shelves are piled high with boxes of K rations, procedure manuals with catchy titles like, "Handling of Deceased Personnel in Theaters of Operations," and medical supplies. He also oversees the motor pool—Humvees and a couple of tanks are parked in neat rows on the back lot.

"How is it going with the camp here?" I ask, sitting in an Army-issue office chair.

"It's not too bad."

Despite the bedlam outside his office, Sergeant Guttierez seems pretty calm. He sits at his uncluttered desk, dressed in fatigues. He's done this before, he explains. Two summers ago Planet Janet shared this military space and it was, he admits, rough going. He describes it in a slow, deliberate manner, putting hospital corners on his words. "The first time it was a learning experience. It kind of was . . . how shall I say . . . ? A madhouse."

Janet and I are sitting on the grass in front of the building, watching happy campers slalom down a Slip 'N Slide. She agrees that it wasn't easy. "Two years ago if we left a speck of glitter on the floor we would get a call, " 'Come back down from Topanga right now and clean this up. Really military, you know.' " She was reluctant to try again, but couldn't find a more ideal space for her camp. The Army Reserve Building sits on the western edge of Veteran's Park, a leafy expanse that features a playground, ball fields, and the Culver City Municipal Plunge. Janet was told by the commanding officer she could use the space, but he didn't want to see "any of those circles with the chicken's feet inside them." We both laugh at the irony. A peace sign is Planet Janet's logo. It is emblazoned on every camper's tie-dyed t-shirt along with the Gandhi quote, "Be the change you want to see in the world."

Janet asked herself how she could "turn poison into medicine" this summer. "We're about embracing everybody, and everybody is different. Victory Over Violence isn't just about saying you shouldn't go to war, it's about winning over your daily life."

I try to think about how I can win over my daily hatred for our president and my anger at his senseless, selfish, deadly war. Georgia said at the dinner table the other night that she wished George Bush would die, and I gasped, realizing I had passed my poison down to my child. We have much to learn this summer, and for all of us, the answer lies somehow with Sergeant Guttierez.

Sergeant Al keeps an open-door policy. Campers wander into his office all day, wanting to look at stuff, ask him questions, help him with his paperwork. Today two seven-year-old girls are trying to do some military push-ups for him. They struggle to push themselves up on their spaghetti arms, but get no higher than the tops of his boots when they collapse, giggling on the floor. When he tells them to focus and try again, one of the girls, feeling giddy and reckless, tells him to "shut his pie hole." There is a stunned silence. Sergeant Al tells her calmly, "It's never okay to talk to adults that way."

Sometimes it looks like Sergeant Al may be going a little native on us. Like an explorer in a strange land, he ventures out onto the drill floor and offers up pieces of his own culture. He cracks open K rations for kids to taste and tries to find a common language with them. He tells them the military is about keeping the peace and that they all really want the same thing. The kids counter with, "We can do that with words. We don't have to do that with guns." Sergeant Al's answer is, "Nobody wants war, but sometimes things must be done."

"We just talk," Janet says with a sigh of satisfaction. "If we can teach these kids how to dialogue now, then later on maybe we don't have to have the war."

When I ask Sergeant Al if the summer has changed him, he says, "Not really." But he admits he's enjoyed getting to know the kids. "In fact, one of the younger boys, for no reason, just gave me a hug when he said hi to me. I found that kind of odd, but comforting as well." In this big, scary, warring, divided world, we have built a little footbridge that connects us. One camper summed up this strange experience in last week's play about Brazilian slave traders: "People are as different as the ocean is wide." This summer Sergeant Al, the kids, Janet, and I have all learned that that is okay.

The Odyssey

It turned out to be the biggest mistake I ever made in my life. Literally, a 4,299-pound mistake made of steel and molded plastic.

It was the first new car my husband and I had ever bought. The salesman handed me a clutch of keys and paperwork and I climbed aboard. I wondered how this vehicle ever got the name "minivan." There was nothing mini about it. As I sat in the pilot's seat surveying the road ahead, I felt more like Captain Kirk on the bridge of the Enterprise than Odysseus on the bow of his ship. Carefully I maneuvered my ship off the sales lot and into space.

I nearly squashed a new VW Bug before I made it around the block. At a red light I pulled up alongside a Chevy Suburban. Our windows aligned and the young man driving locked eyes with me. Then his eyes moved down the body of my minivan, sizing up my ample chassis, and he looked away in utter disinterest.

The first stop in my Odyssey was at my children's school. The kids were, predictably, psyched. They tried every seat, turning the dome lights on and off, overworking the thin plastic of the cup holders.

"Look, Mama!" Franny shouted from the way, way back seat, "There's a secret compartment back here!" I could hear the relentless clicking of the retractable door in her armrest.

"Go easy on it, honey," I begged.

Georgia stood up in her seat to look over the back at her big sister.

"No, Georgie!" I barked. "Don't put your feet on the upholstery!" I took a deep breath and affected a calmer tone of voice. "Please, girls, we haven't owned this car for a full hour yet—let's be gentle with it."

As I buckled them in I experienced a warm pulse of maternal satisfaction. I had done the right thing. I had provided my young with safe and capacious transportation. My precious cargo was protected from the kill-or-be-killed traffic of Los Angeles. The game was survival of the biggest, and I had finally become a player. Now all I needed was the approval of my peers. I set out for my friend Rae's house.

La Cienega was a breeze. The 240 horsies pulled me strongly through traffic. The engine was smooth and quiet. As I peeled out of a green light, I reflected on the irony that my first ass-kickin' V6 engine would be under the hood of a minivan. I had never driven such a powerful car. It seemed to hum all around me, grabbing up the road. I drove like a chauffeur, gliding smoothly into stops, not wanting to age it, harm it, stress it. But in my heart, I knew it was too late. Just by driving it off the lot I had turned it into a used car.

When I turned on to a side street, the going got stickier. A small truck approached, and I saw that, what with SUVs parked on either curb, one of us would have to yield. Since I clearly trumped him on girth, the truck pulled over to let me pass. As I squeezed past him, I felt like a fat lady in a movie theater, trying to gather herself in, smiling apologetically for being so obese.

I pulled up in front of Rae's house and got out of the car with a sigh. From the outside, it really didn't look that big. Rae came out of her house and appraised my vehicle.

"Wow, it's big," she said, standing beside me on the curb.

"I know."

"But it's great!" she went on, sensing my angst.

"Do you think?"

"Sure. It's very practical."

"It is, isn't it?"

"And nice in the green. Better than the gold."

Just then her son, Noah, came out and the look on his face told me that, in his eyes, I was the luckiest person in the world.

"Wow! Cool!" he cried, running up to it and yanking open the sliding door so it went slamming back on its rollers, causing the whole van to vibrate.

"Noah . . ." his mother warned, "go easy."

But Noah couldn't hear her—he was already in the way back with my kids, getting the grand tour. In a second all the rear fan vents were blowing and the dome lights were ablaze.

"Check this out, Noah," Franny enthused, clicking open a compartment between the visors. "This is for *sunglasses.*"

"Cool! This is sooooo cool!" was all Noah could say.

"Well, the kids like it," I observed.

I looked over and saw Rae's Subaru sitting primly in her driveway. A sleek, fuel-efficient reminder of what I could have had if I had chosen what was behind Door Number Two.

My husband and I had spent many hours debating what car to buy. In fact, we test-drove the very car that Rae ended up buying. We wanted the Subaru, but worried that it lacked leg room and cargo space. We wanted the extra seating that would allow us to go places with friends.

At night we lay in bed, trying to predict oil futures and estimate yearly mileage. We looked at our overstuffed garage and wondered how an Odyssey would fit. We fretted that buying such an unthrifty vehicle might send the wrong message to our children about eco-responsibility. The Odyssey also made us confront our family-planning issues. Minivans are for people with more than two children. Did we merit it? Should we have another child just to validate our car choice? Was our family complete? The life issues piled up, making our heads throb.

But then our pillow talk inevitably turned to fantasies of the family vacations that we would take in our Odyssey. The world would open up to us, we would see new places and visit old friends. Like Odysseus, we would be bold adventurers, not stay-at-home Greeks. I saw a future filled with camping and carpooling, bicycles and beach days. Our Odyssey would be a home school on wheels, a laboratory in which our children would learn about the wonders of the world.

You see, the whole minivan yen began with one summer vacation. For a month we lived in upstate New York and drove a rented minivan. We loaded the back of this miraculous vehicle with blankets, lunches, floaties, the little red wagon, and headed off for the lake. The country roads melted away beneath our tires in a blur of lush greenery. We used the van as a dressing room, for changing in and out of bathing suits. We picnicked off the back bumper. It seemed then that life was better with a minivan—more leisurely, more bucolic. It didn't occur to me that life was just better on vacation.

Returning home from Rae's that day, I tried docking the van in our garage. I nosed it in as far as it would go and parked. I got out and hit the button for the garage door. It cleared the back of the van by an inch. I would have to open the door again if I wanted to walk around the back of the boat. Opening the back of the van with the garage door closed was out of the question. A tendril of buyer's remorse sprouted in my heart.

I tried to stay optimistic, but my disdain for the van grew daily, like kudzu. Every time I got behind the wheel I found myself resenting its size, its shape, its airport-lounge upholstery. Like ill-fitting shoes, the van rubbed me the wrong way. It wasn't long before I found myself fantasizing about getting into some kind of accident where no one got hurt but the van got totaled and then I could get rid of it. I prayed for a miracle like grand theft auto, or a nice, low-key carjacking.

What I got, a week later, was a ding. Squeezing into a parking space that was too small, I dragged the tender back right side along somebody's bumper. A deep groove set in right by the wheel well. We hadn't even gotten our permanent plates from the DMV, and I had wrecked the car. I knew my husband, who liked to keep things nice, would be angry. I didn't know how to tell him, so I didn't.

Doug saw the scrape within minutes of coming home from work. I heard him through the kitchen window, swearing under his breath. I made myself busy at the sink.

"How did we get the ding in the van?" he asked.

"What ding?" I said, affecting utter surprise.

"The one by the wheel well."

"Oh my God, I had no idea. That must've happened in the parking lot."

"No, it looks more like you hit someone."

"Oh, but I swear I didn't." This Odyssey was turning me into someone else: I was a lying, minivan-dinging worm. The worst part was, I knew Doug knew I was lying. To his credit, he let it go. But the lie hung in my heart like a rotting corpse.

Which isn't to say the Odyssey didn't bring some good times. Like the time I bought sixteen flats of ground cover from a nursery and folded down all the seats, laying them out in the back. Or the time I blew past a jerk in a midlife-crisis-convertible. Or the time Rae and I piled our four kids in the back and drove down to Adventure City for a day of roller-coastering and Skeeball. I had been right about the things the van was good for. It was good for good times, which I realized were depressingly few and far between.

Mostly, life was about deadheading around town during the day on errands. Every time I drove myself to the Costco or the gym, I thought about all the fossil fuels I was burning just for tighter abs and shithouse-sized packages of toilet paper. I was filled with self-loathing. The Odyssey marked me as a member of the ranks of those I disdained: the over-consuming, overexisting, overentitled American middle class who didn't give a damn who she ran over in her urge to get what she wanted.

The dings piled up. I had always prided myself on my spatial skills. I had learned to parallel park on the streets of New York and was legendary at squeezing into tiny spaces in three points. But in the Odyssey I kept backing up into things: columns, retaining walls, other cars. Before six months were out, the rear flank was dimpled and scratched.

It was lonely up front. Even when the kids were in the van, they were out of reach in the way, way back seat. I would have to pitch juice boxes and pretzels back to them, hoping not to bean them. They would eat, staring out of tinted, fixed windows, breathing recirculated air, listening to Radio Disney and tuning me out as I tried to shout conversation. Sometimes they would spot friends on the road and they would wave mutely behind the dark glass. I would have to roll down my window and relay messages to friends from my frustrated, invisible girls.

We lived in this hell for a full year. Then, one miraculous day, Doug's old Honda Accord gave up the ghost. It was time for him to get a new car. This reopened the car conversation.

"I'd like to get another sedan."

"Okay."

He paused, something clearly on his mind. "Maybe we should sell the van."

"Huh?"

"Don't you think?"

Could I be hearing him right? "Really? Sell the Odyssey?"

"Sure. You hate it. Right?"

"Well . . . 'hate' is a strong word," I demurred.

"Would 'loathe' be better?"

"Maybe."

"We made a mistake. Let's just admit it and move on."

I wept tears of gratitude and joy all over Doug's shirt. Never have I loved my husband more than in that moment. We were going to make a new start together. The next couple of weeks were like waking up from a nightmare. We sold the Odyssey to a childless, retired couple who were overjoyed to have it, dings and all. We bought a nice used Subaru Outback. Driving it off the lot and over to pick up my kids from camp, I felt like myself again. Just a gal in an okay, small, used, pre-dinged car. The kids were delighted with the "new" car, and nestled cozily in the back seat, happy to be closer to their mother. As I maneuvered deftly through traffic, I breathed a sigh of relief. My Odyssey was finally was over. What a long, strange trip it had been.

Sex: Sick!

I am sitting in a dark theater, watching a girl get saddled up by her lover, who stands over her with a riding crop, hard and smirking. Everyone around me is soberly digesting what they perceive to be the film's sexually empowering message, but I am choking on tears and laughter. For that girl could be me, as the director of this film was my first and only sadist.

It was eight A.M. on Sunday back in 1974, and my best friend Gina had slept over. We woke up and padded through the still-sleeping house for massive bowls of Captain Crunch. Then we went up to our clubhouse in the big closet of the upstairs bathroom. We played with our pet rocks, organized our Wacky Packs, hyperventilated each other a few times, and wrote down our hallucinations in the club diary. After a while we got bored and went to hang out on the front stoop.

It was still early, and Ninety-fifth Street was quiet. The house next door belonged to the Baumberg family, a pair of shrinks, and their mean, eleven-year-old son, David. As Gina and I lolled on my front steps, the second-floor window of the Baumberg house rattled open and David leaned out. David was in the fifth grade at our school. He had long, greasy hair, bad acne, and some kind of a pigmentation problem which made his arms and neck look parboiled.

"Hey girls, what's up?" he wheedled from the window.

"Nothing," we answered, attempting an air of disinterest.

"Come over here. I want to talk to you." We walked down my steps and up his. He watched us closely. "Why don't you come in?" We contemplated the stunt. "Come on, I dare you."

Climbing from the top of the stoop over to his second-story window was, I see now, the first risk we took that day. It was a twenty-five-foot drop to the basement level. A little bit scary, but a dare was a dare. In a minute Gina and I had wriggled through the window and were standing in the Baumbergs' study.

The Baumberg study was a hodgepodge of antiques and '70s chrome-and-glass furniture. Bold Gina sidled in next to David on the tuck-and-roll leather couch. Sensing danger, I hung by the door.

Nobody seemed to be awake in his house, either, so we proceeded to amuse ourselves in the manner of preteens, telling dirty jokes, making prank phone calls. The conversation seemed to get riskier with each passing minute, culminating with David saying,

"Hey, I dare you guys to take your clothes off."

"No *way*, David," I said reflexively.

"Oh, come on. You guys are just chickenshits."

"Are not."

"Are, too."

"Fuck you," Gina says, upping the ante with the almighty "f-word."

"Pussies."

"Fuck you!" Gina repeated, and in a trice she was up and doing a bump and grind on the Baumbergs' shag carpet, accompanying herself with a loose approximation of a burlesque song. "Da, da, da, DA, DA, dadadada . . ." David and I watched in stunned awe as she worked her clothes off like a pro. She kicked her feet, sending each of her brown clogs pinwheeling through the air. Then she shimmied out of her dungarees and t-shirt. Then she slipped off her underpants, twirling them over her head before she sent them flying into David's face. At last she stood before us, brown and flat-chested and completely naked. Though I had seen Gina naked a thousand times before, in this context her body held a sophistication that I envied. I could see that she was easy inside her own skin. "Okay, Schickel," she said, stooping to pick up her clothes, "your turn."

I *for sure* didn't want to do this. I was ashamed of my body. It was painfully underdeveloped and rigged like some hideous Rube Goldberg contraption. I was all clanking joints and angles and mismatched parts.

"Nah, I don't want to."

"Oh, come on, Er—I did it."

"Yeah," said David, "you have to."

"No, I don't." I rooted myself into my chair, becoming one with the Naugahyde. There was a long moment where the two of them just stared at me with disdain, and I realized they were right—I had to. The peer pressure was simply too much. I got up and took my place on the shag rug.

I began with my beloved purple sweatshirt, a garment I had worn almost every day for two years. It was my ally, hiding my developing body from what seemed to be an overly interested world. Slowly, stiffly, I lifted the soft, frayed collar over my head. David and Gina went wild, hooting their approval, egging me on. Emboldened, I fumbled with the top button on my brown corduroy pants. I got them undone and down around my knees before I realized I had forgotten to take my sneakers and tube socks off. I had to sit down and yank them off before I could get free of my pants. My face was burning hot but as I removed my undershirt I could feel my nipples hardening with cold under my training bra. I could go no further.

"Okay, you guys, that's it."

"Keep going!!" they shouted in unison.

"Take it *all off!*" David shouted like he was at the OTB.

So I took it all off. My training bra and my underpants, gray and stretched-out around the leg. Every last thread. And when all my clothes were finally lying in a little heap at my feet and I was standing stark naked, pasty-white and big-kneed, shaking with fear and cold in the middle of David Baumberg's living room, the paneled door flew open.

"David? What's going on here?"

I looked up and saw David's mother standing, stunned, in the doorway. Her arms were full of tubes of Christmas wrapping. David leaped to his feet and tried to slam the door. She lost her grip and the tubes tumbled to the floor, like mammoth pickup sticks, jamming the door open.

I jumped up and sought cover behind a . . . table. I tried to hide my great, white, goose-pimply self behind a slender French Provincial leg. Mrs. Baumberg looked at me sternly. "Erika, get dressed and get out of here."

Get dressed. Her words slapped my naked flesh. Naked. I'm actually naked in this woman's living room. *How did I get here?*

I grabbed my still-warm clothes and crawled over to the foyer on my hands and knees, trying to become invisible, to somehow disappear into the carpet. I stood up in the chilly front hallway, untangling my pants legs, putting on my t-shirt inside-out. Gina brought me my shoes and socks. We stumbled down the Baumbergs' front stoop, shoelaces flapping, and we flew up the steps and through my front door, then up two more flights of stairs to the clubhouse, and slammed the door behind us, panting like Labradors.

I needed to write something down about this thing that had just happened. I felt as if my whole life had been cleaved in half. My happy childhood was suddenly over and a strange and sordid adult future loomed before me.

I needed to find words for this crossing. I found a clean page in our club diary and neatly, on the top line, I block-lettered the word "S-E-X." Then I saw myself crouching naked behind that table and my heart convulsed and my brain spasmed with panic and confusion. Suddenly my hand, which had been lying inert on the blank page, sprang to life and spontaneously slashed across the page in big, ragged letters the word "SICK!"

I couldn't bring myself to tell my parents what had happened. I was sure they would disown me if they knew. The next night, my family was walking home from having dinner out, and there, hanging off the Baumbergs' doorknob like a flag of shame, was my purple sweatshirt. The sight made my heart bounce. I prayed we might get past their door without anyone noticing.

"Hey Erika," my sister Jessica chirped, "isn't that your purple sweatshirt?" My parents stopped and looked where she was pointing.

"Oh," I said, trying to affect an air of normalcy, "I must have left it outside when I was playing." I ran up the steps and grabbed it, wondering who might be watching from their windows. In my head I saw Mrs. Baumberg holding my beloved garment between two lacquered fingernails, hanging it on the doorknob with disgust, knowing I would be back for it, knowing my terrible secret.

Gina and I never spoke of that day, which I knew was far worse for me than her. I staggered, exposed and abashed, through fourth and fifth grades. My secret grew inside of me like a malignancy, destroying every good feeling I might try to have, undermining my already shaky, preadolescent confidence. Meanwhile, as we approached middle school, Gina blossomed, becoming accomplished, popular, beloved by our classmates. I, on the other hand, became mute, awkward, swallowed up by shame. As I wandered down school corridors between classes, ever on the lookout for David, my days were a hazy, dystopian nightmare. When I did run into David, he always gave me a pointed look, a look that hissed *slut*.

Just living with my tawdry secret would have been misery enough—but in time, David poured acid on my gaping wound by telling his friends. At first I didn't think he would. I didn't think anyone could be that cruel, but gradually I noticed boys in the grade above me snickering as I approached. Was it paranoia? Then one day I was standing on the lunch line next to Randy Osterow, football player and popular dude extraordinaire, and I heard him under his breath sing the striptease song, "Da da, da DUNH! DUNH! Da, da, da, da . . ." and I knew, I knew that David had told and that the hideous secret I had hoped to take to my grave was now common knowledge. And thus, with little more than the crude tools of the jeer and the sneer, David Baumberg kindled into being my bad reputation. Before I had even made it past first base with a boy, my name was scrawled on the stall door of the girls' bathroom . . . "ERIKA IS A HOAR."

One muggy summer day after fifth grade, while Gina and I were hanging out in my backyard, David spied us from his window and once again leaned out to call to us.

"Hey girls, come over here," he commanded. We obeyed, climbing up onto the wall behind overlooking his backyard. The Baumbergs' yard was a bummer: a barren, asphalt rectangle mined with dog shit. He reigned over it from his window like King Shit of Turd Mountain, an evil sneer on his pocked face.

"There's the little slutties. Hey Erika, have your tits grown yet? Take off your shirt and show me."

"Shut up, David. Just shut up!"

"Why don't you make me? Come on. Take your clothes off right now—I *dare* you."

"Fuck you, David Baumberg! You are just a mean, ugly fuckface!!" I screamed, my skull feeling like it would shatter. David's mother, scowling, appeared at their back door.

"David, close that window. Erika Schickel, I am calling your mother."

Gina and I scrambled back over the fence into my yard and listened for the ring of the phone. My mother picked it up on the second ring and we strained to hear the muffled conversation through the window. All we heard was my mother hanging up and calling out, "Erika! Come inside, please!"

For a brief, panicked moment, I thought I could hide from my mother. I could live like a nomad in our neighbors' backyards, sleeping in playhouses, living on the Pringles and Fluffernutter sandwiches that Gina would bring me. I could make it.

But as much as I feared facing my mother, a part of me also longed for it. I yearned to finally be free of my terrible secret. I found my mother upstairs, sitting on her bed.

"Erika, Mrs. Baumberg just called me. Do you know what she told me?" I shook my head mutely, my eyes burning with two years' worth of unshed tears. "She told me that you and David have been fighting. Is that true?"

"Yes." I mumbled.

"She also told me that some time ago you removed all of your clothing in front of David. Is that true?"

"Yes," I squeaked, my throat constricted with tears.

"Oh honey, why didn't you tell me?"

"Mommy, I was so ashamed. I just couldn't." She patted the bed beside her and I stumbled over and sat down, bursting into so many tears it took several Kleenex before I had settled into a wet, hiccupping mass in my mother's lap.

"Erika, honey, listen . . . when I was your age I did the exact same thing."

"You *did*?"

"Oh God, yes! There was a boy who lived next door, and one day we both got completely naked in front of each other. His mother caught us."

"*Really?*"

"Honey, *everybody* does something like this when they're kids. It's just a part of growing up."

And with those words, my mother set me free. I wept out all of my shame and horror that day as my mother stroked my hair and reassured me that I would survive.

And survive I did. I let go of shame and went on to live a rather shameless life. I didn't think about David Baumberg much for twenty years. Then, when I was thirty-two and a new mother, a filmmaker friend I was having coffee with mentioned with a smirk, "I met an old friend of yours."

"Oh yeah? Who?"

"David Baumberg."

My heart shriveled and quickened under my now large and milky breasts. I suddenly longed for my purple sweatshirt.

"Yeah, he says he knew you in grade school. He told me you stripped for him when you were ten." Two decades later, David was still, pathetically, getting mileage out of this event, trashing me to friends, trying to mindfuck me long distance. I couldn't understand why he couldn't grow out of it. Could anyone really be that mean? What on earth was this guy's problem?

Sitting in the darkened theater in 2002, it all finally made sense. As I watched this unfortunate actress crawl across the floor, I saw myself crawling across the Baumbergs' den, naked and frightened, so many years ago. I realized that after my long humiliation in the fourth and fifth grades, I had finally gotten up on two feet and lived my life brazenly. Thanks to my mother, I had come to understand that there was nothing I could feel that hadn't been felt by someone else before me. That understanding became the ballast in my boat, and I went on to revel in the telling of all my secrets before they could ever again take hold of my soul.

But I realized for David, our experience together had also formed him in some way. I didn't imagine that he was a lamb before that Sunday so long ago, but now I could see that something larger than my own unfortunate circumstances were at work on that dismal day. I had stumbled into the snare of a misogynist in the making. We had somehow shaped each other. But was it possible I had exerted more influence over David than he had on me? It only took me two years to get over that event, but clearly, twenty-five years later, he was still working through it.

As I sat in that movie theater watching his grim little drama that was his contribution to the human conversation, I laughed and laughed. It was the rolling, satisfied laughter of someone laughing last.

Necessary Sugar

It was a seeping, chilly day in early spring, and the wind bit through my purple sweatshirt. We were on our way to see Dr. Weingard, my parents' analyst, and I walked two steps behind my mother down Ninth Avenue. My parents, in the course of trying to save their floundering marriage, were pursuing quite a bit of therapy at the time, the time being 1975. They did group therapy and individual therapy and couples therapy. On this day my mother wanted to do some mother/daughter therapy, and we were already running late.

"Come on, Erika, hustle your bustle." Her own step was full of purpose, and I wondered if something was up, or if she was just practicing her standard Manhattan gait ("step lively, eyes forward, don't dawdle"). We made a quick stop at a bookstore, where she purchased a thick, white-jacketed volume with big, black letters: *Anne Sexton: The Complete Poems*. My mother definitely had an agenda.

We settled into the leather couch in Dr. Weingard's office and once everybody's cigarettes were lit, my mother opened

the book, found a page, and cleared her throat before reading the title of the poem.

"My daughter, My String Bean, My Lovely Woman."

Uh-oh.

"My daughter, at eleven (almost twelve), is like a garden . . ."

Oh sweet Jesus, I could see where this was going. This
was part of the insufferable nightmare motif that was part
of my current life. At eleven (almost twelve), I was in the
full fucking flower of my pubescence, a subject my mother
seemed fascinated by. She was thrilled with my pubescence,
treated it as though it were something happening to her instead of me. She continued on, in a voice trembling with
sincerity, something about a birthday suit and high noon.
Okay, high noon for me was spent hiding my body from my
mother's overinterested eyes. And I had been so careful not
to tell her anything. I lived in stealth, my heart a vault, my
face a blank wall. Where was she getting her information
about *my* "womanhood"?!

If I had to pick a single word from the English language
that made my skin shrink, my teeth itch, and my loins
clench, at that time it would have to have been *womanhood*. What was it about that word? It whispered of femi-
nine secrets and righteous propriety. Womanhood is a
pastel sigh, moist eyes, toilet water on pulse points. It
comes with a brood of ugly smaller words clinging to its
skirts: puberty, tampon, vulva, gift. *Why must the vagina
words be so awful?* I so often wondered. Why couldn't my
mother be reading me *The Wreck of the Hesperus* or *Ode
on a Grecian Urn* instead?

The next stanza was a blur of globular lemons, engorged garlic buds and swelling apples too hideous to even repeat. Can we leave my lemons out of it, please?!! God, are ALL mothers this unbelievably embarrassing?

Yes. I see now that we are. The things I do that turn my own children crimson include public displays of goofy behavior, singing in accents, laughing too loud, saying exactly what I think the minute I think it. Half of it I am unaware of until I see the pained look in their eyes.

As a mother, it is my duty to discuss sex with my daughters, but I have chosen the opposite tack from my own mother. She had a way of making sex talks Very Special Events. I remember the first time we had "the talk." She sat us down at the dining room table with a nice dessert and explained the facts to me and my sister like this:

"The man puts his penis . . . (wooohooooohoooo!) . . ." she said this in mock, kidlike alarm, "into the woman's vagina . . . (yeeeewwwwwwy!) . . ." and so on.

Her sound effects were no doubt intended to acknowledge and diffuse our embarrassment at the subject matter, but instead it was the genesis of my embarrassment.

When talking to my kids about sex I do all I can to keep it casual and matter-of-fact. An anti-Hallmark Moment. I try to treat the facts of life as though they were nothing more than . . . well, the facts of life. In my casual outlay of information, my hope is that I am neutralizing the subject. Talk of sex, puberty, and birth are not momentous, special bonding occasions, it is just part of the conversational weave of everyday life. It is just information, and all questions are always welcome. So far, it seems to be working.

"Look, Mama, I've got breast buds!" Franny exclaims, directing my attention to her swelling nipples. At the tender age of ten (almost eleven) my firstborn daughter is beginning to come into the flower of her own womanhood (I blame the hormones in the milk!).

I wish I'd had *The Care and Keeping of You: The Body Book for Girls,* a paperback Franny bought with her own money. The book lays out the pubescent body in nonthreatening, user-friendly terms. "I'm Stage Two, Mom," she informs me, pointing to the line drawing of a naked girl brushing her teeth in a bathroom mirror. The pen-and-ink sketch is simplistic and bright. This is simple, Saturday-morning puberty, whereas mine was a dark midnight full of confusion and loneliness.

The caption beneath the drawing reads, "A raised bump called a *breast bud* begins to develop under each nipple." *God, I so could have used that information*, I think. When I started to bud, I didn't know that the hard discs beneath my nipples were normal. I lay in bed at night, anxiously palpating the raised bumps in my otherwise flat chest, not knowing what they were, but worrying that I might have breast cancer. *Was it possible for ten-year-old girls to even get breast cancer? How long would I have to live if I didn't get a diagnosis? Can you even do a mammogram on an undeveloped chest?* I should have gone immediately to my mother to assuage my fears, but that thought was even worse than the thought of silently wasting away from my double tumors.

When I got my first period I was at my dad's new bachelor pad. There was *no way* I was going to tell him, so I just stuffed some wadded-up toilet paper into my underpants and waited until I got to Phoebe Schlossman's house, where I was sleeping over. I told Phoebe, who told her mother, who threw a pad at me and yelled, "Mazeltov!" This was perfect. No fuss, no tender words to shine the way toward my future fertility. Just a big, fat mouse mattress between my legs and a bowl of chocolate ice cream in front of the TV.

The poem ground on endlessly. I was dimly aware of a stanza about watching her baby grow inside her magical, ripening belly. This was exactly the problem. I mean, was nowhere safe from my mother's prying eyes?

I didn't know then what I know now; my mom's interest in my changing body wasn't so much prurience as proprietariness. She had made my body with her own, and naturally she felt a vested interest in its current state of flux. She had explained the birds and the bees to me, armed me with Kotex, taken me bra shopping. She simply wanted me to share it with her. *No!* I wanted to scream at her. *It's mine! You can't have it!!*

On the other hand, I was perfectly willing to share my body with anybody else who was interested.

> *"And someday they will come to you,*
> *someday, men bare to the waist, young Romans*
> *at noon where they belong,*
> *with ladders and hammers*
> *while no one sleeps."*

Someday they will come? The Romans had already arrived. Men (and boys), sometimes bare to the waist, but more often wearing black concert t-shirts, were climbing their ladders already. They were spinning the bottle, leering at me on the street, copping feels, wolf-whistling. A camp counselor had tickled me and put his tongue in my mouth, and the owner of the neighborhood comic book store had taken me out to an R-rated movie in midtown. Though these Romans had yet to scale my parapets, I could already see their greasy heads cresting my turrets.

What details my mom left out of her sex talk, I filled in by reading. Not only did I devour the requisite Judy Blume books—but I read *Fear of Flying* and *The Joy of Sex,* both available on my parents' bookshelves.

As I poured over the erotic illustrations, I dreamed someday of having a zipless fuck. I was more than a curious, precocious thirteen-year-old, I was jailbait waiting to happen.

Most of Franny's friends are interested in boys. The fifth grade is abuzz with rumor and innuendo. "So and so has a crush on so and so." Her girlfriends think Antonio Banderas is a *hottie.* Franny rolls her eyes at this. She still sees her boyfriends as boy friends and has them over for sleepovers. Boys like her because she likes to play Legos and Foosball and doesn't care that they are boys. She blushes when I ask her if she *likes* likes anyone. "No, I just don't think I'm ready for that," she answers sensibly.

By thirteen I was galloping down the road toward sex. My parents were two years into a vicious separation and deeply involved in their now-swinging love lives. My father was emulating *Love American Style* with a series of "lady friends" that I mostly never met. My mother had chosen Gina's dad as her next partner. Gina reacted by forevermore cutting off all contact with me, even at school. With her pretty singing voice and cool older brothers, she skyrocketed into middle-school popularity, while I festered in loneliness, confusion, and unquenchable anger.

Left to my own devices, I began to fail school, filling my lonely afternoons not with homework, but in assignations with eighth-grade boys. It was a late-70s, pre-AIDS New York City. Everyone was having sex, it seemed. Why not me, too? Given my psychological profile at the time (precocious, unsupervised, insecure), it only seemed right that I went looking for love in all the wrong places. After school I would ride the bus home with Randy Osterow. We would get jacked-up on Cokes and Chocodiles, then retire to his football-themed bedroom to make out ferociously until his parents got home from work.

One day, after an hour of spitty fun, Mark peeled off his jeans to reveal his cock, pointing due north on his hairy belly. It was large, salmon-colored, terrifying. I jumped up and ran into his bathroom, locking the door behind me. I sat on the sink and sobbed, watching the tears rolling out of my startled eyes. Who was I? What was I becoming? Was I ready for this? Was there any way I could go back to what I had been five minutes previously—a fast girl with no real information or meaningful contact with the opposite sex? Or would I have to go out there and touch Mark's penis, thereby pushing over the first domino and initiating the chain reaction that I knew would lead to the loss of my virginity within a year and sealing my deal as class slut? I dried my eyes and went back out to push over the domino.

Okay, maybe Sexton was right, women are born twice. The years between Franny's two births are now a faint ladder of pencil marks on my kitchen doorjamb. She stands! She talks! She reads! A whir of inches and new shoes. Her body, as it grew, was always my responsibility. I kept it clean and fed and warm. But now she is taking over the reins. She brushes her long hair carefully, keeping it neatly behind her shoulders. She cuts her own nails, and last week she got her ears pierced. At first I balked at the idea. I thought she was too young, but who was I to say? This was her decision, not mine. I kissed each virginal lobe before she got into the chair, scared but steadfast. I stood back and let a strange woman punch holes in my child. All I can do is midwife at this second—birth, Franny has to give birth to herself.

I understand that at a minimum, the point of raising children is getting them to adulthood in one piece, but I'd like to retard their growth a little. Or maybe just do that special effect in *The Matrix* where everything freezes and you can walk around the diorama of your life, wiping up the spilled milk before it hits the rug, kissing the soft cheeks of your babies before they squirm away into their next incarnation.

There was a time when I was impatient to see the next stage. I would look at Franny's baby face and search for clues as to what she would look like when she grew up. Now I see it, in the lengthening of her jaw, the rise of her nose, the changing scent of her skin. The body is clay. It is shaped by time and our own will. It is drawn out and thinned by the years. She will be a lithe and lovely woman, possessing great warmth and beauty. The Romans will rush to her.

Before the Romans conquered me with their rude hands, it was my mother who touched me. I tingled when she gave me hairdos, and when I was sick with fever she would rub cool witch hazel into my body. These rubdowns made me want to stay sick. It was quiet and my hot skin absorbed her every cooling stroke. The witch hazel smelled like hot dog water to me, almost edible. My sheets would be slightly damp and I could feel my body cooling and relaxing under her touch. In my catalogue of sensual memory, this is my first.

"Rub my tushy, Mommy, rub it," Georgia coos, raising her naked butt in the air. Georgia, the hedonist in our family, has always been the cuddle monster. At seven, she is still dependent on me to satiate her deep hunger for touch. I run the palm of my hand over and over her sweet cheeks until my arm grows tired. It is my pleasure and my privilege to do this. But also, it is my duty. Because if I don't touch her, then who will?

Georgia's favorite place in the world is my lap, and her body still fits easily into mine. But Franny, never as cuddly as her sister, has even less need for my touch now. She is long and awkward and can only perch on my knees for a moment before the circulation in both our legs gets cut off. She still needs a good-night kiss and craves the occasional back scratch, but her body is outgrowing its instinctual hunger for my body. Her lovely bones need their space. She is becoming her own.

My tall, statuesque mother, her voice wavering with emotion, reads a stanza about how she will always be there, a steady old tree in the background. An old tree in the background? Ha! I am no more ready to take on that role than my own mother was thirty years ago. But already I feel gnarled and deeply rooted. Fell me and you will see the rings of my past, new skin growing over each phase, reflecting changes in the weather and conditions of life. These are the rings of childhood. This was the year I was a vegetarian. Here are four cold winters spent in the Berkshires. This is from the era in which I loved Jim. Here are my many sweet years with Doug. Here are my girls—my heartwood.

I long to be a sapling again. On the cusp of middle age, I feel alien to myself. All my life I have been green and flexible. I was beautiful every day. I could not walk to the corner without stirring longing in some man on the street. I inspired valentines and turned heads and made men wish I was older. Six months after I had Franny a man paid me fifty dollars to let him suck my toes in a bar. Sex was never not a possibility for me at any time, and even though I happily settled down to have sex with just one man, I led a life buoyed by mojo.

Then something happened. I turned forty and it was as if I had gotten a mojo-ectomy. Guys who would once have stopped to flirt now walk right past me without so much as a backward glance. By dint of living I had lost my foothold on foxy.

I think a woman is born three times. Though I'm not even peri-menopausal yet, I can see where this is headed. The long, sweet flower of my youth, the one my mother tried so mortifyingly to shepherd me into, is doing a slow wilt. Next stop, years of sensible shoes and hormone replacement therapy, where you either cling desperately and unbecomingly to youth, or elevate to a higher plane, unfettered by obligations of estrogen and vanity. Sexton calls it "necessary sugar."

"I'd like to tap that" is something men are saying these days when regarding a pretty, young girl. At first I thought it was a spigot/keg reference, taking a long draught of beer. But now I think it has more to do with sugaring. It's the sap they want. Green and pungent, sticky and pure. The blood of saplings, viscous and full of life.

The idea of some Roman wanting to jab his spigot into my sweet girl makes me reel with anxiety and sickness. Could my mother have known what was around the corner for me, back in 1975? Of course she found out later when she read my diary and threw in the towel by sending me to boarding school. She told me I was a danger to myself, and also to her. I was thirteen years old. She moved out west, taking my sister with her and leaving me on the East Coast to fuck my way through the last leg of my childhood. When you chop me down and look inside, the darkest ring is from the year she let me go.

By the '80s my sugar had been tapped and spilled and bled out of me by boys who didn't know how not to hurt, and men who only didn't want to get caught. I have tried to count my many Romans, but I cannot remember them all. Some had sweetness of their own to offer me, which I lapped up gratefully.

I don't look back on my early sex life with regret. It was a rich adventure that finally led to Doug, the one man who wanted to tap the good in me that I had come to doubt. His sweetness was of a kind I had never known. Out of this simple syrup we made our girls.

> *"Darling,*
> *stand still at your door,*
> *sure of yourself, a white stone, a good stone—*
> *as exceptional as laughter*
> *you will strike fire,*
> *that new thing!"*

My mother gave me the book at the end of our session and I have hung onto it all these years, its white jacket now tattered and yellowing. Over the years I have come to learn more about Anne Sexton, how she only spared moments for her daughters between madness, brilliance, and pathological narcissism. The irony of my beautiful, fiercely intelligent, hyperbolic mother giving me this book as some kind of talisman makes me laugh now. I wonder if this poem haunts Linda Sexton as it does me, a little too much a little too late. A wild gesturing from a woman on the shore, growing ever smaller as we drift away.

And yet this book (the first book of poetry I ever owned)

has became my unlikely friend. It ushered me into the world of poetry, a world I came to love. Though my mother and I have disagreed about many things, we have always believed deeply in the power of words.

Every day I repeat incantations over my daughter: "You are good, you are smart, you are strong, listen to your heart, use your head, (clean up your room)." My faith is that this magic will help her hang onto herself over the next decade or so, until she finds her place in the world without me.

Somehow, in the end, I made it through puberty and into myself. Along the way I learned that a woman is so much more the sum of her ever-changing body parts. Then why, as the male gaze is turned away from me (to fall too soon upon my own daughter) do I cling to the "womanhood" I once so abhorred? Who can I hope to be when my sap has dried into amber? A white stone. A good stone. As exceptional as laughter.

Potluck

I was unloading Georgia's backpack, sorting through the jumble of empty drink bottles, her badly rumpled Brownie vest, and various important school notices that had gone out of date when I came upon a crumpled notice from her teacher:

ATTENTION PARENTS: On Wednesday, November 23, the second grade will host a multicultural potluck. please have your child bring in a dish from your family's country of origin.

Fuck me. Of all my parental duties, and this would include taking my kids to the doctor for shots and watching "Veggie Tales," there is little I dread more than the multicultural potluck.

Of course, here in the spicy goulash that is Los Angeles, they are a nearly annual event. L.A. is a veritable rainbow coalition of Tupperware enthusiasts and the multiculti potluck is the Ziegfeld Follies of home cooking. Everyone trots out their auntie's baba ganoush, or their grandmother's mascarpone recipes, and the exotic dishes glisten with oils, arrayed under rainbows of colored Saran Wrap. Most beautifully, each dish strengthens that child's sense of heritage and cultural identity.

For my children, the multicultural potluck is confusing and mysterious.

"Let's bring in pizza!" Georgia suggests when we discuss the upcoming event.

"Why pizza?" I ask, wondering if she thinks we're Italian.

"Because . . . you're from New York," she explains with a "no-duh" lilt. Apparently she thinks of New York as a nationality unto itself, which, of course, is exactly how New Yorkers see it, too.

"Honey, I just grew up there, but that's not where our ancestors are from."

"Oh, then where are they from?"

"Well, my side of the family goes back to Europe—England and Germany. Daddy's family is also from the British Isles—Scotland, England, and Ireland."

"So what dishes do we have?" she asks, so reasonably.

"Well, meat pies and blood sausage, haggis and jellied eels, and, of course, there's black pudding."

"What's that?"

"Well, I think its pudding made with pig's blood."

"EEEW! That's disgusting!" Georgia shrieks. She doesn't even know the half of it. How do I tell her that as White People, we come from a long line of racists and crusaders, slave owners and oppressors. Yes, we have Shakespeare and Churchill, and a host of other cultural poster boys, but basically we are the people of blood and icky meat dishes that I don't know how to prepare.

That night, Georgia, Doug, and I are lying on the bed,

further considering our potluck possibilities. What if we were to take a more national tack?

"My family is from the South," Doug suggests. "You could make fried chicken,"

"Yeah, fried chicken!" Georgia enthuses.

Doug's family tree sports ancestors named Earl and Wyatt, Southern dirt farmers who stare out of sepia photographs with flat, pinched faces. Though no one in Doug's evolved, fair-minded, liberal immediate family has ever said so directly, I've sometimes wondered if there isn't a little Klan in his clan. It just so often comes with the territory. Though racism has thankfully been bred out of the family bloodline, their taste for chicken-fried steak and marshmallowy sweet potatoes endures.

The foods my husband's family eats are more foreign to my Eastern, citified palette than hummus and vindaloo, which I practically grew up on. My Manhattan childhood was all bagel smears and take-out Chinese. The first time I was introduced to Doug's family was at Easter. After years of dating Jews, it was my first sit-down Goyisha meal in over a decade. I missed the matzo, I longed for the hiroset. I was utterly taken aback by a milky, pinkish Jell-O dish that was served alongside the ham. And yet, these were my people. We were all WASPs, were we not? I should have been at home there among the dinner rolls and candied yams. Why did I feel so misplaced?

"Mommy, make fried chicken!" Georgia says, bouncing around on the bed.

"Fried chicken? Guys . . . I'm not exactly known for my Southern cooking." I throw a leg over Georgia to still her, and she starts to sulk beside me. I've never made fried chicken one single time in my life and am not at all versed in grease cookery. I can make a nice Waldorf salad. But that's just another dish from the country of New York.

* * *

My mother's people were Methodists who pioneered the Pacific Northwest. My father's family can be traced directly to the *Mayflower,* a fact that my grandmother reveled in. Before she died she bestowed the family archive on me— boxes of crumbling genealogical documents that her father had painstakingly gathered when he wasn't Shrining it up with his lodge cronies. Every year my grandmother traveled from Wisconsin (land of the three-meat buffet) to Plymouth, Massachusetts, to frolic and eat game with the other WASPs of the Mayflower Society. When I came of age she proudly added my name to the rolls of the D.A.R., for whom she worked her entire life. We are the very whitest of the White People.

Now I find it is my cultural duty to bring a dish, the food of my culinarily uninspired people, the people who were too busy invading countries and slaughtering brown-skinned innocents to think up any good dishes or use an ingredient not found on four legs, and set it among the bright offerings of those whom we have historically oppressed: Georgia's schoolmates.

"I know—why don't you just bring in some nice baloney sandwiches on Wonder bread," Doug suggests, only half joking.

"Too much work. I was thinking more along the lines of Cheese Whiz on crackers."

Of course, the obvious choice would be to roast a turkey, but this potluck is scheduled for the very day before Thanksgiving, which I am hosting this year. I'm already cooking a turkey and am in no mood to do it twice.

In fact, the whole potluck thing is making me very, very cranky. Why are the second-grade teachers burdening us with additional shopping and cooking the day before the biggest shopping and cooking day of the year? And then I realize that many of the families at our integrated school won't have to participate in this bland, American holiday claptrap. They came to this country to be free, and will be off enjoying their hard-won freedom at the latest Harry Potter movie as I'm wilting in the kitchen over a steaming pot of mashed potatoes.

The multicultural potluck is designed to be inclusive of all the people who have been left out of the dominant, Anglo-Saxon culture the American calendar is set up to honor. And yet . . . why do I feel so left out? What is Thanksgiving, after all? Initially it was a day where we gave thanks to our Native American friends for helping us so that we might live to kill them off and steal their land another day. It's been a gravy train for us ever since, and for this we continue to give thanks. How do I explain this to my child without spoiling the fun?

"But *Mommy*," Georgia implores me, "what will we bring?"

I decide on shepherd's pie. Not real shepherd's pie, mind you, with minced lamb and leek and a host of other ingredients toxic to the seven-year-old palette. Besides, who has that kind of time when Thanksgiving looms? In the spirit of the Midwestern branch of my family tree, I make a nice, bland version featuring ground turkey and some frozen vegetables with a lid of instant mashed potatoes. The next day I reheat the Pyrex dish in the teacher's lounge microwave and set it out on the lunch table, a comestible cinder block amid the other bright, savory offerings of the potluck.

The feast is glorious. It is an international smorgasbord of delights: tortillas, black beans and rice, baklava, kimchee, a garlicky pasta primavera, homemade challah, and chana masala. I load my paper plate until it sags, and Georgia and I gorge on the foods we have grown up with. I sit as far away from the shepherd's pie as I can, hoping no one will associate it with me. When the potluck is over I find my dish, which has been stabbed at a little, but is otherwise un-eaten. I rewrap it and take it home.

"Nobody ate this?" Doug marvels, looking at the shepherd's pie in the fridge. It is one of his very favorite dishes. He takes it down to his family's Thanksgiving gathering that weekend, where it is a big hit.

The Fucking Cat

I am making out with the tatoo guy from yoga. We are sticky on his mat, and he is peeling off my sweaty Lulemon top and there is a Buddhist monk ringing a chime over and over and over and over.

We get into the plow posture and I am just about to reach Nirvana when the rhythmic chime becomes a whine. An annoying, repetitive whine. I open my eyes to my predawn bedroom, its peach-colored walls not yet awake to sunlight. The whine is the familiar nagging meow of Buster, our family cat, sentried beneath the window closest to my side of the bed.

"Fuck you, Buster," I mutter. Clamping my warm, damp pillow over my head, I try desperately to weave myself back into the frayed edges of my dream, but Buster's rhythmic whine slices through the duck feathers and goose down like a chainsaw through bubble bath.

He does this every morning. After a night spent prowling the backyard, he wants to get back in before the dew falls. Fair enough. But after months of getting out of bed to let him in the back door, we finally cut a big hole in our house and installed a cat flap so that he may come and go as he pleases. A nice, Plexiglas portal which, if you get down on your hands and knees on our back porch, affords you a good view of the toilet in our second bathroom.

But does he use this flap? I don't know if it is simple sadism or colossal stupidity, but Buster keeps insisting on us getting up to let him in the back door. In either case, I have come to hate the family pet.

Up until the flap went in, Buster had engaged my family in a complex game of open sesame. He would park outside the den door and meow until I got my TV-watching butt off the sofa to let him in. This happened roughly fifteen times a night. At first I graciously complied with his wishes, trying to follow rapid-fire *West Wing* dialogue as I opened and closed the door, my patience ebbing. By *The Daily Show* I would find myself slamming the door behind him, catching the tip of his tail and sending him yowling out into the backyard.

Buster has a spectacular tail, a fluffy flag he holds high over his lithe, black-and-white body. From a distance, he is a rather magnificent-looking tuxedo kitty. His blacks and whites are strikingly laid out. But if you get up close, he's a mess. His black spots are randomly spritzed with white. Sloppy work. "Buster is a good idea, poorly executed," my mother once observed.

"Rowr? Rowr? Rowr? Rowr?" It's not so much a question as a challenge. He knows I hate him and this is his revenge. The subtext of every plaintive yowl is, *get your sorry carcass out of bed, you bitch*. Ordinarily I am a reasonable person, able to let the cat in and go back to sleep, but he does this *every night*, positioning himself under the window by my side of the bed, meowing for as long as it takes to get me up.

It is one thing to spoil my good night's sleep, quite another to sabotage a good sex dream, and indignant rage surges within me. I shove back the covers and plant my feet heavily on the floor, half hoping it will wake my husband, but he sleeps on. I galumph through the house, softening my steps as I pass my daughters' bedroom door. I get down on my hands and knees in the spare bathroom, cursing the cold tile of the floor, the headache that is blooming behind my eyes, and the day I thought it would be nice to have a pet again.

Doug is the one who chose Buster out of a pile of homeless kittens at the shelter. Since getting a cat was my idea, I wanted him to pick which one. I felt it would be some insurance against him blaming me if it didn't work out.

Doug lives by the Ignatius J. Reilly ideal of "the right geometry and theology" in all things, including cats. As we watched the tiny black-and-white kitten hop around on the shelter table, his wee tail quivering with ferocious ambition, I'll admit I liked him, too. He seemed to possess a lively spirit. Whatever. We had dragged our kids to every shelter in town, looking for the right animal, and I was ready to wrap it up. Let's just get the fucking cat already.

I am a cat person. Growing up, our family always had at least two pussers in the house. Being apartment dwellers, dogs were never a pet option, which was fine with us. I loved our cats: their kneading and purring, their velvety toe pads, the musk of their fur heating up under reading lamps. Cat love is flirty and surprising. When dog people accuse cats of being aloof and uncaring, I want to scratch them.

In college I missed the company of a cat, so I adopted

one of my own. Pushkin was a prince among cats. An orange tabby with a head the size of a honeydew melon and wide paws that sported opposable thumbs, Pushkin was a gentle giant with a retinue of charming quirks. He so loved to be petted he would buck up on his hind legs, raising his giant head to meet my hand. His meow sounded like "Mgap!" and it made me laugh every time. Pushkin's only flaws were his taste for houseplants and his profound disinterest in grooming. His heavy orange coat would shed and waft across my parquet floors like downy tumbleweeds. It was part of his mellow overall personality and I didn't mind much.

Pushkin chaperoned me through college and several jobs, serial dating, and celibacy. We moved from apartment to apartment, and then to California. Upon meeting Pushkin, Doug said, "Why, he's the Harrison Ford of cats," and it was true. Bluntly handsome, simple and sweet as a pound cake, Pushkin had star quality. The three of us moved in together.

Things got serious between me and Doug. We were inspired to make a family of our own together, so we adopted Hazel, a calico female. She had chocolate and toffee-colored markings that made her face look like a Picasso, and a louche coat that would make Cruella DeVille swoon. She was, however, as mean as she was beautiful. She snipped and scratched and preened. This, paired with her superior smarts, captivated our respect and affection. Hazel could fetch rubber bands and bottle caps, yet always dictated the terms of the game. She loved to play in water and would sit on the edge of the bathtub to splash in the faucet. When she was feeling magnanimous she would curl her body around your neck like a living stole.

Pushkin mostly kept his distance from Hazel, but sometimes we would catch him washing her. For grooming-inept Pushkin, this was a stirring act of love.

Hazel's tragic downfall was her asthma. She would lay her throat against the floor, Hoovering her head back and forth, wheezing elaborately. We took her to a vet, put her on steroids, bought an air filter for our apartment, then, finally, took her to a cat acupuncturist, all to no avail. After several years, Hazel was gasping for every breath and had to be put down. Pushkin died a year later of severe old age and, I suspect, loss.

I hold the cat flap open and peer out into the murky dawn, calling to Buster in my sweetest voice, "Here Busty, Busty. Come on, Buster." Buster scoots into view and peers at me mistrustfully through the short tunnel that separates us. I try to read his eyes, but can barely see them, as they are lost in the black of his face. Is he afraid, or just mocking me? It's impossible to see behind his mask. Pushkin's eyes were like golden dinner plates, serving up the all-you-can-eat buffet of his soul. But Buster's dark eyes are obscured, unreadable, untrustworthy.

"Come on, Buster," I implore, my voice saccharine and fake. I am the witch in the gingerbread house. I want nothing more than to get him inside and then stuff him in the oven. Buster sniffs the opening of the hole.

We hadn't had Buster for more than a few weeks when I realized something was wrong. Not only was he strangely bipolar in his affections, coming out of hiding for petting, then biting me when I did. But he was also a nag. If his crunchy bowl were to get low enough as to see the white of the dish at the bottom (while still being ringed by a pile of food), he would come and whine at me until I filled it in. When I sat at my desk working, he would jump in my lap and demand active, constant petting. When I pushed him off to type, he would jump back up until I finally had to close the door. After a few weeks of this I came home one day to a fresh pile of turd in the corner of my office. After the fifth time he crapped in that corner we finally had to have the year-old carpeting pulled up.

Of course, I knew what he was telling me. He wasn't happy with me. But why me? Why was I the locus of his neurosis? Here I had two perfectly lovely, energetic children ready to indulge his every need. Could he sense my reluctance? Was he, like all those who suffer low self-esteem, magnetically drawn to those who disdain him?

Indeed, Buster seems most drawn to those who can't love him. When Rae comes over he moons around her legs, begging for attention. She can't pet him, either, as she'd bring the dander home to her allergic husband. This only seems to make Buster want Rae more. I think it's safe to say that Buster has some co-dependency issues.

"That's it, Buster, come on in," I coo out the bathroom portal. He reaches a tentative paw forward and I resist the urge to grab it and yank him into the house. In the dining room the cuckoo clock chimes five A.M. There is only an hour and a half before the kids will be up, clanging their spoons against their cereal bowls, bickering and dawdling before school. I need that last ninety minutes of sleep, or I will be crusty and tired for the rest of the day, short with my children, good to no one.

Buster puts his head in the tunnel, and I continue to croon, "That's it, you stupid motherfucker. Come on, you piece-of-shit cat, get into the fucking house before I kill you."

My hostility toward this creature startles me. I want this cat out of my life. But how? Frances is fiercely bonded to him, making cozy little nests for him and writing him love notes. Her affinity for animals, the weak, the injured, and the friendless is the root of her being. I cannot account for how such a pure, sweet, empathetic being sprang from my own sardonic, cynical, selfish flesh. But Franny is the only one in our family who would be devastated by losing Buster. Georgia loves him, too, but only when she really thinks about him, which is not very often. But sending Buster back to the shelter would break both their tender hearts.

It's our fault he's like this. In the beginning, when we first brought him home, my children were younger and more rambunctious. I think Georgia terrorized him with her boisterous, four-year-old energy and high, squeaky voice. He went from being a friendly, playful kitten with his tail held high to a cat who slunk behind the sofa whenever people were around. Loud noises cause him to bolt. The slam of a door, the roar of a helicopter over our house (a nightly event), even the crinkle of a grocery bag makes him skitter sideways out of sight. Good friends react in surprise if Buster makes an appearance—they didn't even know we had a cat.

At first, I petted him a lot. But every time I put my hands on him he would get frisky and eventually claw and bite me. My pale hands soon were scrimshawed with tiny scratches from these encounters. Gradually I stopped trying to pet him. It didn't matter much, as my hands were constantly occupied with the petting of my children and the myriad household tasks that kept me overoccupied. I figured he was getting enough attention from the girls, who doted on him obsessively, squealing and chasing him under furniture. Little did I know that their overzealous love, combined with my indifference, was turning him into a sociopath.

The fact is, Buster brings out every small, petty, aggressive, murderous, unkind fiber of my being. He's the catalyst for all my latent evil. The greater my coldness, the more needy and neurotic he becomes. During the day he only sleeps on my side of the bed, leaving a mulch of fur and dirt on my pillow. When I am on the couch he comes and presses his cold nose into my neck, begging for love. At first I am happy to pet him, enjoying the silky nap of his fur, but either he gets overexcited and starts to nip, or he butts into me over and over again. When I relent and pet him he gets more worked up, turning around stiff-legged in my lap, tickling my nose with tail fluff, presenting his quivering anus. I beg him to sit, to curl up in my lap and snooze, like every other cat I have ever known has done, but Buster is a gaping wound of neediness. He demands my undivided attention. If I wanted to give constant attention I would have gotten a dog, or had another kid. Cats aren't supposed to be co-dependent. I grow angry, I feel invaded. After fifteen years of sharing my body with a husband and two kids, I just want some space. I don't want anybody else begging for my attention or my touch. This is my time to be alone. I am just tapped out. I try to explain it to him: "Buster, I need my space." He presses his head into my hand for more petting and I sit on them, denying him what he craves. "Look, it's not you, it's me," I tell him, like the unfit lover I am.

I always thought that I was a person with an unlimited supply of love, but now I see how miserly I can be with affection. That this animal is the catalyst for this revelation makes me flush with shame. He stares up at me, expectantly, still not getting it, waiting for more, so I try the gold standard of breakup lines: "I love you, Buster, but I'm not *in love* with you." He butts at my forearm, trying to coax my reluctant petters out from under my thighs. This enrages me. "Leave me alone, you crazy motherfucker!!" I scream. Startled, he shoots off to an undisclosed location. We are both stunned by my hostility. Which came first? The bitch or the cat? It's as though we created each other.

I have been crouched on the bathroom floor for ten minutes, and my mind ranges over possible Buster disappearance schemes. In the state of California, I am told, you can be arrested for killing a dog, but not for killing a cat. It has something to do with the fact that dogs are seen as domesticated animals and cats are wild. I could just let him out in front of my house and hope he gets hit by a car. I could toss him over the back fence and let the neighbor's big dogs have their way with him. I could throw him in the trunk of my car and drive him up to the Hollywood hills and leave him for the coyotes. It would be so simple. Oh God, I am a monster.

Then, like a miracle, Buster pokes his head in the flap and reaches another paw through. He seems perplexed by the logistics, and in fairness, it is a small passageway for such a big cat. I midwife him through it, grabbing his paws and pulling him in like a breeched baby. Once his back legs are through he shoots past me, knocking over his water dish, and disappears into some dark corner, no doubt to avoid the evil he so justifiably fears. I pee, then head back to my bedroom to get one last hour of shut-eye. But who is curled up on my pillow, enjoying my scent and latent body heat, and shedding dirty fur? The fucking cat. Back in the day I would have curled around my cat and gone cozily to sleep, but the bitterness is too deep. *I don't think I have enough humanity to love this animal,* I think as I toss him off the bed. I have failed in this relationship.

I try explaining it to my friend Lou, who is a cat person. He and his wife have four cats, upon which they dote.

"Have you ever had just a really bad cat?"

"Nah, how can a cat be bad?" he asks, genuinely.

"It's just that Buster is so all-or-nothing. Either he's completely in my face, or hiding under the bed. He's leaving turds in my office. He's neurotic and awful. Doug and I are seriously thinking about taking him back to the shelter." I am trying this out on Lou, taking the idea's moral temperature.

Lou frowns at me. "You know, I was given away, so that idea just really upsets me." I love my friend Lou for a variety of reasons. He's a brilliant chef, an informed conversationalist, nerdy, worldly, achingly funny, and as sweet as the ocean is deep. The miracle of Lou, though, is the fact that he spent his childhood in a series of loveless foster homes, where his many gifts went unappreciated, to say the least. His beautiful spirit prevailed nonetheless and he emerged from his horrific upbringing one of the finest, dearest people I have ever known. When I look at Lou, the rescued boy, I feel like a malicious, backhanding, stained-undershirt-wearing, "bring-me-a-fucking-beer-you-piece-of-shit" swearing foster parent.

I go back home to Buster and try again. I try to see the Lou in him. I try to rise above my own expectations of what a cat should be and love this one for what he is. I reach for some Hallmark-like aphorisms such as, "Everything happens for a reason" and "God doesn't give us more than we can handle." Though I don't believe in God per se, I do believe that some force in the universe is telling me I need this animal now. There must be some instruction for me in this relationship. Buster is going to help me rise above my own limitations in love. He will help me to expand my capacity for empathy and humanity.

For a time, things are better. We reach a truce. I find things to love about Buster. He's pretty. He's only an animal, incapable of malice. He can't help it that he's an idiot. I get out the brush and spend hours grooming him, working him up into a blissed-out frenzy. I make sure there is never a white space at the bottom of his bowl. I coo his name and chirp happily as I open the back door for him umpty times a day. Franny notices the change: "It seems like you and Buster are getting along a lot better, Mommy."

"Well, I'm trying. I really am." Franny hugs me and we both love me a little more.

Then he pees on the couch.

Not only does he pee on it, he pees on the spot that I favor. The side with the reading lamp, my lap blanket, and my knitting. This is not an accident, but a full-on act of war. I sop up the urine, air out the cushions, and refocus my efforts on forgiveness. But he does is again. And then another time.

A pissed-upon couch is not simply a mess to clean up. It is a lost couch. It is landfill. There is no way to get the stink of urine out once it has soaked down to the frame. This is the last straw for Doug, who has assumed most of the clean-up and cat maintenance and is less consumed by guilt than I am. He, too, has gone from love to loathing, and longed to be free of our *bête noir et blanche*. He has even less compunction about hauling Buster's ass back to the pound than I. But first we have to explain it to the children.

"Buster isn't happy here," we tell them, and their chins start to tremble. It's not like they don't know what's coming. They are exquisitely attuned to everything that goes on in their home.

"You don't like Buster! You've never liked him!" they accuse us.

"That's not entirely true," I lie. "We've tried to make it work, but we think he just isn't happy in our house. It's too noisy. He's scared of everything. It's not fair to him."

Franny is silent and still. I can hear the sadness echoing down the deep well of her soul. I can hear the splash of tears at the very bottom in her voice. "But what will happen to him if we give him away?"

"Well, I don't really know. But we can keep tabs on him through the shelter's Web site, and make sure he gets adopted."

"But who will take him?" Georgia asks in a wail.

"Hopefully some nice, single lady will take him. He'd be so happy in a quiet house, with one person who really loves him."

Franny looks at me, tears slipping out of her big, wide-set eyes, "I understand, Mommy. It's the best thing for Buster. We have to do what's right for him." I see that the lesson I am going to learn isn't coming from Buster, but from my own daughter, who knows more about love than I ever will.

The next Saturday we put the sofa out on the street, and take Buster to the pound. He is given a serial tracking number which is put in the computer. Franny leaves a small bag of toys and a note with instructions for the next owner on what Buster likes and dislikes. The girls bid tearful farewells and everyone is heartsick. We come back to an empty house, forlorn but free.

The next day Doug calls the shelter, as he promised the girls he would, to see if Buster had been adopted. Buster is still there. He has two weeks to get adopted or he will be destroyed, though of course, we don't tell the girls this. We pray for that mythical nice, older, single lady. The one with piles of catnip toys who will stitch his name on petit point pillows and feed him fresh chicken off her plate. If she doesn't come, then what? In spite of my murderous fantasies, I suspect we'll end up readopting him. I cannot live with his blood on my conscience.

Two days later Doug calls the pound and they tell him a

woman came in and fell completely in love with Buster and adopted him on the spot. He is saved. We celebrate, happy that Buster is free of us at last. We go couch shopping. We buy the girls hamsters. Though it is not one of my proudest days, it is among my most joyful.

Foot Notes

Pre-Op

Dr. Hong holds my foot tenderly in his warm, sure hands. He explains the procedure again, gently trailing his fingers along the contour of my bunion; he will make a three-inch-long incision, then cut the bone, realigning it into the right direction, and insert four long, steel pins to fuse the bones back into the correct position. "There will be some discomfort," he tells me, and I think, *Discomfort? No problem. I am a strong woman. I've had two ten-pound babies. I can handle some discomfort.*

Dr. Hong looks into my eyes, smiling warmly, and says, "I like to treat my patients like family. If you have any questions or problems, I want you to call me, day or night. We are in this together."

I feel like the luckiest girl in the world to have this capable, bow-tied, clean-scrubbed, honor-student-faced doctor taking care of me. Choking back tears of gratitude, I sign the necessary release forms. Then we hug.

Running Away

Eight months earlier I was sitting in a Subway restaurant, eating yet another "7 Under 6" turkey sub, feeling the bland, murky commingling of low-cal ingredients on my tongue, and a bland, murky lack of enthusiasm for life in my heart. I watched my kids plowing through their turkey subs, just trying to get to the cookie at the end, and it felt like a metaphor for my whole, predictable, sedentary, bland, middle-class existence. Where was I going? What were my goals? Now that I had had my children, what was left in my life to do that was extraordinary? That's when my eyes miraculously fell upon a stack of pamphlets for "AIDS Run L.A."

It was a marathon to raise money for AIDS research. It would take place in Chicago, a great city I had never seen. And these nice people at AIDS Project L.A. would train me, get me through it, and reward me with a nice tote bag and a free t-shirt. That was all I needed to sign up.

The next six months of my life were spent running. Running and running and running. I would get up at five in the morning, leaving my children with their father, their babysitter, whoever was on hand, and go run for miles and hours. The endless pounding of my feet on the pavement shook my brain loose from the hamster wheel it was on, and put me on a whole new hamster wheel. One where I calculated distance, time, and hydration needs. I acquired a taste for nutritional gels and savored mouthfuls of energy bars that tasted like cocoa-flavored cuticle. I pretty much hated every minute of it, and yet I was overtaken by an insane need to accomplish this insane thing. I wanted to do something mighty and extraordinary and completely out of character. Doug and the girls simply had no interest in it.

I went to Chicago and ran that fucker. I proved to myself

that I could do anything. Nothing could hold me back. I roared across the finish line exhausted, caked in road dirt, and mighty. Then I sat in the grass, wrapped in a foil blanket, and wept. When I got home the next day nobody patted me on the back, or hung a banner, or even asked me how the race went. I just went right back to making macaroni and cheese. All I had to show for my stint as Wonder Woman was a tote bag, a t-shirt, and the mother of all bunions.

Reality Bites

Surgery is fun! I am naked beneath a thin sheet. People in masks gather around and are very busy with important tasks, all intended to benefit me. I say, "It's chilly," and they insert a big, fat blow-dryer tube up under my sheet and shoot warm air all over my goose-pimply flesh. Then handsome Dr. Hong appears. I wouldn't have recognized him if it weren't for his kind, confident, almond-shaped eyes above his surgical mask. I am calmed by his presence. The anesthesiologist has just painlessly connected my IV and asks if I am okay, and I say, "Mmmmm," as the molecules in the air above me become visible and perform an intricate ballet.

I wake up numb and cozy under a blanket and I am wheeled into recovery. Still so sleepy. Nurse gently tries to rouse me, which is a tad annoying, but I'm so happy under my blankie. My foot appears to have been worked on, and is swaddled like a papoose at the end of my leg. Everything is hunky dory. After a while I am rolled through the hallway on my bed. Whee! We get into an elevator that smells of warm chicken.

"Yum, yum, lunchtime," I coo to the fluorescent tubing

above me. I could do this every day. I'd like to stay forever, but I am an outpatient. So they send me home.

On the doorstep of my house, I begin to feel some of the discomfort Dr. Hong spoke of. But really, it's no biggie. I hobble into bed awkwardly and take a Vicoprofen, obeying Dr. Hong's advice to medicate before it gets too painful. I am a good patient. I am going to bounce back from this quick as wink, I think as I nod off to sleep.

I am awakened two hours later by a growl of pain in my foot. Within minutes I am moaning on my bed and writhing like a hooked fish. I take another pill, which knocks me out entirely.

I awake to my friends Teresa and Kimberly, who have brought me food: a huge pan of lasagna, a party bowl of salad, and a loaf of garlic bread. Enough to feed my family for a week. I am hungry and indulge myself in a feeding frenzy. There will be no calorie-counting for me now.

Pain, pain, pain, pain . . . more pain. The pain, oddly, is not on the side of the foot on which I had surgery. It runs like napalm along the outside of my foot, shooting into my baby toe.

The day darkens into night, and a series of TV programs waft past my unfocused eyes. At eight P.M. I can't take it. I page Dr. "Call me Jack" Hong. He calls me back from a hockey game, his voice laced with impatience.

"What's up?"

"I am in so much pain," I sob, but in the din of the Staples Center, he can barely hear me. I can tell he doesn't want to have to pay attention to me, and it stirs some old anxiety in me. I hate having to inconvenience him. Begrudgingly, he agrees to call in a prescription for codeine. I dispatch Doug posthaste to the local Sav-On to pick it up.

All the codeine seems to do is make me sleepier, more

groggy, which makes it more difficult for me to do the one thing which I have found eases the pain: get up and walk around a little. But every forty minutes, the dull pain grows into a point; I must get up and ambulate dizzily around my bed, flushing my foot with fresh blood and buying myself another forty minutes of shut-eye. Sunup finds me draped over the tops of my crutches like wet wash, watching the sky lighten, weeping piteously as I haul my exhausted carcass around the room one more time.

My girlfriends return and are shocked to see me so unimproved. "This isn't working. You need stronger drugs." They go home and search their own medicine chests for expired prescriptions from long-ago C-sections. They call and rouse me momentarily from self-pity into a bracing state of consumer dissatisfaction. This doctor is not providing an adequate service! There's no reason for me to be in this much pain! I page him again, feeling mighty in my self-righteousness. I sit back on my pillows, testily awaiting his return call.

The phone rings, startling me out of a perfectly lovely Chris Noth dream, and a voice says, "Hi, Erika, how ya doing?"

I hesitate, confused. "Good . . . who is this?"

"It's Jack."

Jack? Jack my ex-boyfriend in New York? Nah. Jack Black? Jack Sprat? Okay, I give up. "Jack who?"

"Jack Hong."

"Oh . . . Hi!" I am completely taken aback. I didn't know we were such pals. Wait a minute, we're not. Why is he calling me? My foot throbs in answer.

He's returning my page. He is in Kansas City, lecturing, and is in no mood for my pity party. He tells me that anything stronger than Vicoprofen is a triplicate drug and he doesn't like to have his patients too doped up. I say, "Look, all I can do is lie here—what does it matter if I'm insensate?"

"Have you ever taken any drugs?" he asks with a curl of suspicion. "I mean, recreationally."

Ever the good girl, I answer dutifully, "Well, I have smoked some pot."

"People who have used narcotics recreationally often have trouble feeling the effects of prescribed narcotics." Does he think I'm a drug addict trying to get a fix?

"But cannabis is not a narcotic!"

To this statement of fact he replies, "What do you want me to do? Undo the surgery? You are going to feel some pain." His sarcasm feels like a slap. I am not good at confrontation. I don't want to make him so angry that he'll give up on me.

"Okay. I'll be okay."

"Okay!" he says, clearly cheered that this conversation is about to end. "Call me any time."

At my first scheduled Monday appointment, Dr. Hong begins removing the dressing to look at his work. As he slowly unwinds the yards of wrapping, I feel like a character in a soap opera, waiting to see her redone self. I am curious, yet afraid to look at my new foot. As the last of the dressing comes off, my husband, who has stalwartly witnessed the birth of our two babies, catches a brief glimpse, blanches, and has to leave the room.

It is a Frankenfoot. It is swollen many times past its usual size and has steel bolts coming out of it. It is the shape and color of an eggplant. My foot is no longer my own. It is a piece of raw meat on a surgical steel rotisserie.

"It looks good!" Dr. Hong declares, and I take my big, tender foot home, wrapped in nothing more than a whisper of gauze and an Ace bandage. I feel more vulnerable than I ever have in my life.

Bored and feeling sorry for myself, I call my mother in New York for sympathy. "Poor baby," she coos. "I wish I could be there to take care of you, to bathe you." This statement strikes me as utterly preposterous—the idea of her sitting next to the tub looking at my grown-up, broken-body makes me recoil.

"Oh God, I can't think of anything worse!" I blurt out. It's thoughtless comments like these that wound her the most. I am dangerous for her, she has said, and it's true. I am toxic and insensitive.

I decide against leaving the house altogether. It's too scary. So I stay in bed, eating Vicodin when the pain spikes and trying to negotiate domestic life on crutches.

The "no-duh" problem I discover on crutches is that you are never hands-free when standing or moving, which had never really occurred to me before. Carrying anything, especially anything liquid, is impossible. On my first weekday alone at home my devoted husband is pulled from my side by a heavy workload at the office. My children/personal servants are at school. I have no one to bring me water. I lie in bed, panting with thirst. I drink out of the bathroom tap when I get up to pee.

Then I remember the canteen. I manage to dig it out of our stored camping gear and fill it up. I loop it around my neck and head back to bed.

At the end of the week I am feeling a little better and moving pretty fast on my sticks. I feel determined to get back to enjoying my busy lifestyle and deny my handicap. I have been invited to a "Goddess Party," an all-girl event featuring food, booze, and sex toys. Starved for fun, I arrive at the party and do a nosedive into a Cosmopolitan. I find a comfy seat and drain my Cosmo. When I get up on my crutches to mingle, I get the spins.

I suddenly feel utterly vulnerable and horrified to be out in the world. What was I thinking? All that stands between me and another surgery is an Ace bandage and one wobbly leg. Drinking is out of the question. What is a Goddess to do?

I retire to the safety and comfort of the sofa to watch the karaoke singers. My bad leg is crossed over the good, my maimed member dangling limply from my ankle. I feel protected by the coffee table and don't notice the big house canine coming up to nuzzle the cheese plate that is set in front of me. Roused by a salami two trays down, he muscles past me, shouldering into my foot. As the pain gyrates up my leg, I am terrified, positive that I have made a mistake in coming out. I rush home like a guilty teenager, reeking of booze and smoke, and quietly put my foot to bed.

The next morning I am tired. I help Georgia get ready for a party, and as I am leaving her room I place the tip of my crutch on a silky dress-up lying on the wood floor. The crutch flies out from under me and I crash to the ground, landing awkwardly on my foot. I am gripped by fear. I have done the worst thing possible. I quickly call Jack Hong's emergency number and wait for him to return my call, moaning and trying to gauge the damage I have done. What if I have dislodged a pin, or broken something? He will have to reopen my foot and redo the surgery. I am crying when he calls me back. He tells me I'm probably okay and to ice it. If I broke something I'd know it and he'll X-ray it at our Monday appointment.

Having escaped the worst, I vow to be more careful. I keep my radius smaller. I stay in bed devouring entire novels in three big bites. I watch so much TV I can feel my palm grafting to the clicker.

I venture out of the house once a week to see my shrink, where I sob out my agony. It seems that I have big issues around asking for or accepting help. Friends and family call me up and offer to do favors—laundry, cooking, shopping. No matter how desperately I may need this assistance, my standard response is, "No, I'm fine. It's okay. I'm okay. No, really, I'm good." I can't admit that I am felled, hurt, unable to take care of anything. I can't believe that they really want to help me. I'm sure they secretly resent me for my helplessness and they are covering their resentment under a sheen of kindness. Underneath, they suspect I am milking this for attention. They think I should stop moping, pull up my socks, and get back in the game.

Socks. Oh, how I miss them. My left toes shiver in the chill morning air of the California spring. I long for soft, woolly, snuggly socks. I dress my foot in a bandana because I know the sight of steel pins protruding from flesh freaks people out. Kimberly looks at my rig and says, "Girl, I don't care how many pretty scarves you wrap around your foot, that shit is *still* ugly!" Yet I feel it's so much better-looking than an Ace bandage. Hong laughs as he unties my bandana to inspect my foot. He says I should market the wrappings. A person could make a killing in this area. If only I gave a shit.

Even though I do nothing but lie around all day with my foot up, the stress is killing me. All the things that I enjoy in life—exercising, gardening, cooking, carrying my sleepy children into bed—none of these are available to me. I am what I do, and without a functioning body, I am slowly becoming lost to myself.

There is, in fact, no physical pleasure for me, but for the

pleasure of the vibrator I bought at the Goddess party. It's a tiny thing, wrapped to look like a roll of Lifesaver candy, with the slogan "It's a Life-Saver!" scripted on the side. I am using it liberally for medicinal purposes. I lie in bed and imagine Dr. Hong unwinding a bandage that covers my whole body. I come so hard I reinjure my foot a little.

When I was young, there would always come a moment in my illnesses when my mother had had enough. I could feel her patience for me ebbing, like a warm tide moving offshore. This would be my signal to pull it together and get better. I have always been good at knowing when enough was enough. I have given myself two weeks to recover from this surgery—then I will trouble the world no longer with my selfish needs.

It is seven minutes past six and my husband is not yet home from work. My kids are tired and hungry. Poor Doug has to do everything. It would be so nice if I could have dinner started.

I head into the kitchen and fill a saucepan with water for pasta, a four-part maneuver on crutches, during which I spill a little on the floor. I cannot see the puddle against the hard, white tile, and, of course, I put my left crutch down into it. My crutch flies out from under me and I do a triple salchow, landing hard on the tile floor. I have just delayed my healing by another two weeks.

This fall precipitates an even harder fall into depression. My whole family is suffering, and it's my fault. Georgia, almost four years old, misses her mommy. I have been replaced with a pathetic, bitter invalid. This makes Georgia very angry and she rages against me all day, every day. My husband, behind in his work, goes back to the office after he puts the kids in bed. He is exhausted and testing the limits of his antidepressants. Left alone, without any adult supervision, I, too, turn to drugs. I find some dried crumbs of weed at the bottom of my stash can and smoke them, but they provide little succor. When I am not lost in a haze of Vicoprofen, I cry and write anguished foot poetry on my laptop.

It is two o'clock on a Saturday, and Target is crowded. I approach the row of electric scooters parked by the register and consider my options. In the past I have scoffed at the people who drive these. Lazy people, fat people. I feel sheepish as I ask the cashier for the key.

I tuck my crutches under the steel railing that separates the carts from the cashier island, praying that some sadistic practical joker won't take them while I shop. I choose the cart closest to me and hop aboard. I put the key in the ignition and the battery gauge lights up with a good charge. I cannot hear the hum of the motor over the din of the store, so I put it in reverse and hope for the best. It snaps backward with a thin, high-pitched, ladylike *beep, beep, beep*. It has the backup beep of a pink Tonka truck. In the high-speed whir of Los Angeles car culture, the Target gimp-mobile is the solid bottom of the pile.

I jab at the forward arrow and the cart pitches forward, in the direction of ladies' accessories. *God bless the Disabilities Act,* I think as I surge into the stream of shoppers, rejoining the consumer culture I have so missed. I am halfway across the main aisle when the cart stops dead. I switch the engine off and on again, and it surges forward another three steps, then konks out completely. I am a good fifteen paces away from my crutches and the other carts. This tiny distance is insurmountable for me. I am utterly stranded, in a sea of able-bodied people. Tears spring to my eyes. I will either have to ask for help or crawl across the floor to my crutches. I spot a red-vested Target employee trying to re-store order to a shelf of purses that had been ravaged by shoppers.

"Excuse me?" I call. She stops what she's doing and looks up. Then she looks down and sees me on my dead little scooter. "Hi," I say in an apologetic tone, "this thing has stopped." She gives me a confused look. "It's broken," I clarify. Her face tells me she understands, but still doesn't know how to respond. "Could you either get my crutches, or bring me another cart?" She is more confused. I hand her the little silver key. "Another cart, please?" We make eye contact and she takes the key from me and goes to get me another scooter.

In the bathtub I regard my hoof with wonder and dis-taste. It has been dangling, untouched and unwashed, for a month. *So this is what happens when you don't wash.* It is covered in a yellow crust of smelly, dead skin. My incision makes the swollen foot look like a busted bolster cushion that has been taped back together. My foot cries out to be bathed, so since the rest of my body is in warm water, I lower my foot into the tub. Then I start to rub it with my washcloth. As I rub, layers of skin come rolling off my foot. I feel a spasm of pleasure and satisfaction at this. I roll more off with my fingers, then with a small loofah. Half an hour later my work is done. I have exposed a soft, pink, healthy, and loved foot. I take it out into the garden to dry in the sun. The afternoon breeze against my tingly skin is deli-cious.

The next day the incision begins to weep, oozing an amber liquid that looks like tree sap. I sense my foot is let-ting go, turning a corner. I need more of this kind of atten-tion. Holistic, Eastern. I need nurturing.

At the Santa Monica Homeopathic Pharmacy a helpful

pharmacist loads me up with a number of homeopathic remedies to aid healing. I leave with several small, brown glass vials that seem to be filled with the same sugary pellets that came in the doctor kits I played with as a kid. I eat them like candy and the next day I develop a strange itch, which quickly turns into a fullblown rash.

The rash is on my ears, my eyelids, my neck and face. It crawls up my crotch and into my armpits. I am driven insane by the need to scratch, and without knowing it, I scratch open the sores and they bleed. I am in total, unmitigated *hell*.

It is three A.M. when I am finally driven from my bed by the itching. I draw an oatmeal bath. As I lower my shining, red hide, one-legged, into the tub, I find myself submerged in a memory. I am six years old and have gotten into the poison ivy that grows in the woods behind our house in Washington Depot. Mommy made a bath like this for me, in the claw foot tub, in the long bathroom of our old house. I remember the setting sun in the open window, a late-afternoon breeze blowing in. Mommy is sitting on the edge of the tub, testing the water, talking to me. It is heaven, being in her gaze, talking like grown-ups. Why have I failed at this relationship? Where did that trust go? What made us turn against each other?

I have failed at healing. I thought I would be the best one at it. I had imagined Dr. Hong saying things like, "Wow, you're an amazing patient!" My husband, who, during my marathon training, dubbed me "Amazon.mom," has never seen me like this: demoralized, self-pitying, completely unable to rally. All the reference points for who I am have gone missing.

Alma begins needling me. First, a tiny prick in the tops of my earlobes. A gnat bite, nothing more. Then she needles my legs. Again, tiny pricks on my right leg, what one could accurately call "discomfort." Then she says, "Okay, I'm going to do your left leg now." She places a needle in my ankle and the length of my leg ignites with pain.

"Oh man, that hurts!" I cry out, gritting my teeth until the fire dies down.

Then she says, "Okay, cough!" I do, and she jabs another needle into the top of my foot and I am rocketed into a dark cave of distress and grief. I begin sobbing, hot tears sliding into my ears. Alma holds my foot and lets me cry. "Poor baby," she says, "poor baby. There is a little girl in there who needs to be taken care of. Help her." I suddenly feel like I am six years old again, and I cry until I am finished. Alma leads me into a relaxation, describing a soothing light that fills my entire body. Then she tells me to imagine that my mother is as big as my thumb. When I do, she has me put my tiny mother into a pocket over my heart.

Hong told me he wouldn't take the pins out on Monday unless I'm somewhat walking. So I try, try, try. I am comfortably standing and am practicing an awkward stride while supported by crutches. It hurts, but in a good way. Both girls have birthday parties that Saturday and I take them to the first one at Build-A-Bear. One of the dads there is a physical therapist, and he asks about my recovery. When I tell him I had surgery six weeks ago, he is shocked. "You should be walking by now! At least walking on one crutch."

I am ashamed. Have I been lazy? Too timid? I toss a crutch into a corner and proceed to lurch around the party, helping the kids pick out names and outfits for their new bears.

By Monday morning my foot is throbbing and I start to freak out. I wonder if here, in the eleventh hour, I have broken my foot. Will I have to go back into surgery and have my foot reopened? I take a long bath, which causes me to begin sobbing. I cover my face with a washcloth and begin praying to the God who watches over agnostics for help. "Please, please, please, let me be okay," I beg, tears sliding into dirty water.

Dr. Hong is in his little darkroom, developing the X-rays. He comes back in, puzzling over the first.

"Well, this one looks okay . . ." he says, his face a mask.

"Are you saying the other one looks bad?"

"No, I haven't looked at the other one," he answers testily. I back down. Sometimes I think he phrases things deliberately to make me worry, but I would never dream of telling him so. He peers into the ghostly image, divining my fate. He places the picture on a light board and I can see the long screws embedded in my skeleton, making right what my relentless running had made wrong.

That morning I had photographed the screws in my foot, first against bathtub tile, then on grass. I had gone in six weeks from utter horror at the sight of that rig sprouting from my skin, to an odd familiarity with it. It had become a part of me, and that is what Dr. Hong said was causing the pain. The bone was growing around it.

After an agonizing silence, he says, "It looks beautiful—let's take out the pins." My heart leaps with joy and fear, and an odd touch of sentimentality. He starts unscrewing the pins slowly. At first I don't feel anything, then I feel a sharp jab as the tip of the screw withdraws through bone. As I gasp, Dr. Hong stops, but I beg him to keep going. I want to get it over with. Like childbirth, I am so wanting the outcome that I almost don't mind the pain.

It has been a great foot day. A day out and about with my family, looking for a kitten, going to the park, winding

up with tacos at Gilbert's. At the end of it my husband and
I marvel at the slimness of my unswollen toes. We are all
tired, and after one story, Georgia is ready to snuggle down,
but first she needs "Baby Mexico," a baby doll we bought
for her south of the border. I get up from her bed and hop
across her room to the doll shelf. No, not there. Perhaps the
toy box? I hop over and land on something that impales my
right foot. I collapse to the floor, twisting my left ankle and
screaming in pain. Doug rushes in. I have searing pain in
both feet and my mind becomes unhinged. I am crying and
cursing uncontrollably and my children are sobbing in horror as they watch. He turns on the light and I see that my
foot is bleeding badly. I look where I stepped and see the
jagged little crown that came with Georgia's new Cowardly
Lion Ken Doll. You know the scene in *The Wizard of Oz*
when the Tin Man smashes a pot to make a crown for the
Lion? This is an exact, hard plastic replica of that. Doug
quickly gets a paper towel for my right foot and a bag of ice
for my left.

Now I cannot walk at all. Each time I come close to recovery, I am plunged back into infirmity. Why? What is it
that keeps me here, in this physical limbo, held back from
the rest of my life?

Lying in bed, I take a series of phone calls, first from
Teresa, who tells me I need to "let go." This is what my
therapist and my acupuncturist have been telling me. "But
let go of what?" I ask her, sincerely wanting an answer.

"I don't know. Let go to God?"

"But I'm an agnostic. I don't think I have enough faith In
God to do that."

"Yeah, maybe just call it a higher power." she suggests
unhelpfully. The rhetoric of recovery always makes me

squirm. But I know that something in what she says is true. I need to let go of something to get better. My mind and body are hanging onto hurt.

The next call is to my sister. I recount the crown injury and instead of sympathy, she reprimands me for doing too much. She tells me that I have to stop doing things—I cannot hop around on one foot. The first feeling I find is anger, defensiveness. "I feel like you're judging my healing." She says she's not being unsympathetic. She says she's all sympathy.

"I'm on your side," she says.

"Until you've lived on one foot for two months, you can't possibly understand my side. I had to get that baby doll down for Georgia."

"Yes, but Erika, you need to *hold on to something*." Her words gouge me into a hollow yawn. I can feel wind blowing between my ribs. *You need to hold onto something*.

Let go. Hold on. Let go. Hold on. My brain swirls with the yin and yang of this puzzle. I need to let go of this old pain so I can hang on to the support system I have created. My friends, my family, my own inner strength. As I am puzzling this through, I stumble across a memory:

I am standing with my mother on the corner of Eighty-eighth and Madison. Blacker & Kooby Stationers is across the street. We are going to buy pens and coloring books and I jump off the curb to run over there. My mother throws her hand across my chest, holding me back on the curb. Then she slides her hand down my arm and grabs hold of my hand. But there is no car coming—I had already checked. "The light is green, Mommy."

"I know. I can't help it. I guess I'll protect you for the rest of my life." Naturally, I took her at her word. But now, all these years later, I see that she couldn't possibly keep that promise, any more than I could keep it for my own children. Life just has too much pain to offer. It will come and snatch your mother away from you, even as she struggles to stay by your side. She will be sucked into her own pain and leave you to try and cope with yours. Like Georgia, I am raging against it. I am angry and sad and scared. I have held on to myself all these years, proving to everyone that I am all right, when really I am not. I have overcompensated for my vulnerability and fear by running marathons, making jokes, clinging to my faith that everything will be okay in the end. It is this stubborn mindset that has kept me from healing, because I refused to be broken in the first place.

I look down at my swollen, punctured foot resting on the bed. I hold it tenderly in my warm, sure hands.

Dr. Hong is pleased with my recovery. The holes where the pins were have scabbed over, and everything seems to be healed. He writes me a prescription for physical therapy. I need to learn how to walk again.

In one of our initial consultations Dr. Hong told me that his mother, who still lives in China, has bound feet. I was amazed that such cruelty still persists, and I endowed this fact with a moving story line about how witnessing his mother's torture inspired young Jack Hong to be a healer of misshapen feet. I felt it would make him more empathetic to the distress of being unable to walk. Now I see it was nothing more than an interesting and lucrative career path for him. I don't think he has any idea what I've been through in the last two months, nor do I think he particularly cares. Eight weeks ago that would have made me hurt and angry, but now that our journey is almost over, I feel a surge of love and acceptance for him. He can't help the way he is. In my mind's eye, I make him the size of my thumb and put him in a pocket over my heart.

Fire Escape

"Smoking was never cool. *Smokers* were cool."
—Malcolm Gladwell, *The Tipping Point*

I am a burner. Cigarettes, joints, pipes, cigars, cloves, bidis, candles, sage sticks, incense, firecrackers—if it can be lit, toasted, or inhaled—I want it. I have a serious craving for smoke. I like my cookies burnt, my marshmallows scorched, and the fireplace a conflagration.

My fingers itch to kindle. I burn to coax flame out of wood or paper. I search out-of-state supermarkets for boxes of "Strike Anywhere" matches so I can strike them anywhere—on grout, brick, or stone. I savor that tiny explosion with its heady musk of sulphur.

I covet fuels. When in the countryside, I collect kindling, loading the trunk of my car with nice, dry sticks to take back home. I have some almond wood and a few logs of piñon two seasons old that I am saving, like a vintage wine, for a special occasion.

I can spend hours watching wood burn, dreaming of what fuels I will add next, thinking about how the air is circulating between the logs. I like putting my whole head next to the flame and blowing on it slowly and gently, a fiery fellatio—feeling the heat rise in my face. I view a juicy bed of glowing coals as a goal in and of itself. I can coax just about anything into flame with one match: wet wood, soggy twigs. Basically, I am one gas can shy of total pyromania.

I offer this information as partial explanation for why I am so drawn to smoking. A burning ember at one's fingertips? Joy! But it's more than the bliss of having a lungful of smoke and smooching off a halo of perfect smoke rings. I also love the busy-work of smoking: rolling a joint or cigarette, lighting up, tapping the ash, paring down the ember when my butt has gotten hot-sticked. I crave the smell of sulphur and tobacco mingling in that first drag more than any other part of a cigarette. I love to flick a butt and watch it arc through the air before it lands in sparks on the asphalt.

About fifteen years ago my non-smoking sweetheart (soon to become my non-smoking husband) convinced me that cigarettes really are a disgusting habit, and that if I wanted to live happily ever after with him, I would have to give up gaspers for good. He had no objection to the sultry aroma of burning reefers, however. In fact, Doug shared my view that pot was stupidly illegal, that it was a happy, harmless quality-of-life-enhancer. And though he kept his own tea-smoking to a once-a-year event, if I chose to bone up a couple of times a week, he was quite okay with it.

So here's what I did: I substituted marijuana for tobacco. I could light up and puff away just like the old days. In many ways it was even better. The taste and smell is better. The paraphernalia is better. Bongs, pipes, clips, one-hitters, many crafted of beautiful, swirling art glasses (most of my childhood I dreamed of growing up to be a glass blower—again *fire*). I loved the crumbling, the rolling, the lighting, the tamping, the burn, the smoke, the smoke, the smoke. So this is how I became a pot head.

Burn, Baby, Burn

But let me back up, because really, my jones started long before I got married, which was actually the midpoint of my smoking career. I began, innocently enough, at ten, by filching cigarettes out of my mother's purse. They were little more than an accessory for pretend. Gina and I would drape ourselves over my bedroom furniture, ciggies aloft, imitating the gestures and cadences of our smoking parents. We sickened ourselves on my mother's Trues, and once I reached the considerable age of twelve, I was ready for a new challenge.

In sixth grade, Gina and I were at a school mixer with our friend Reese, a persnickety rule-follower. The three of us were huddled on the girls' side of the gym, trying to act like we weren't checking out the boys on the other side. Our lips glossed to a mirror sheen, teetering on our Cork-Eez, we observed one of the boys, loose-hipped and skinny in a Stones t-shirt, separate himself from his friends and make the long trek across the basketball court and approach us.

"Hi, I'm Lowell," he said, looking straight at me. "Wanna dance?" After four minutes of a slow, bungling shuffle, Lowell let go of my clammy hand. "Wanna smoke a joint?" he asked casually. I knew what a joint was, though I had never laid eyes on one. I was dying to get a visual.

"Yeah, sure!"

I imagined a joint would be just that—something crooked, hinged, possessing a right angle of some kind. I was surprised when Lowell withdrew from an orange prescription pill bottle a skinny, white cigarette. We went outside onto the schoolyard, hid behind a backboard, and smoked it. I didn't get high. But I went back to my girlfriends and told them I did get high, and that was a high in and of itself. Reese, shocked that I would do something so, so . . . *illegal,* huffed off in a fullblown, pillow-chewing twit. So deeply satisfying was her reaction to my drug use, I decided I would try to make it a habit.

The Salad Days

Finding dope in New York City in the 1970s was easy. In those pre-War On Drugs days, a girl could nab a nickel bag on her way home from school as easily as picking up a candy bar.

My dealer, Jesus, a black guy in nylon overlap pants, was so skinny he looked like a cardboard cutout. He hung out in front of the Azuma on Eighty-sixth Street, muttering, *"Sense, Sense, Sense"* to passersby. Too young to know that he meant *Sensimilla* or to know what that was, it was nonetheless abundantly clear to me he was a pot dealer. With but a few strategic words and a week's worth of my allowance, he would retrieve a dolly-sized Ziploc bag from on top of a nearby parked car's tire and slide it to me. For a thirteen-year-old whose mother still took her shoe shopping, this was commerce on a wildly heady scale. With my drugs tucked into the skintight back pocket of my Gloria Vanderbilt jeans, I could pop by my favorite newsstand, pick up the latest issue of *Howard the Duck,* a Charleston Chew, and a pack of Zig-Zags and be set for the afternoon. Pot in those days was green and crumbly, not all souped-up, sticky buds like it is today. I would twist up a lumpy, pregnant joint and smoke it in the fire stairs of my building before retiring to my room to listen to Billy Joel and ignoring my family until dinner.

Understand, the high I got continued to be in the act itself. I didn't really inhale—nobody had ever showed me how to hold a hit. I didn't even know that there was a word for the little stub of joint left over, that I would shove behind the fire extinguisher. The pot was certainly not *Sensimilla,* more likely oregano. But I liked the act of smoking it—the secrecy, the paraphernalia, the feeling that I had a life of my own that nobody else knew about. I was engaged in the classic adolescent pursuit of trying to become a creature apart from the one my parents had reared.

Pot was definitely a gateway drug, but not to other drugs. Rather, it gave access to a private world of secret behavior and limitless possibility. I started cutting school in order to attend matinees of French films. I felt I learned more about life from *The Lace Maker* and *Mon Oncle* than I could possibly learn in seventh grade. I shoplifted at Bloomingdale's and Saks Fifth Avenue, taking mirrored scarves and bright, wooden bangles that I could wear on my solitary, incognito adventures. All of this was my way of demonstrating that I was now officially the boss of me.

In eighth grade my mother found my poorly hidden diary and spent the afternoon reading it while I was in school. In a rare parental meeting, she and my father decided I had troubled them long enough.

I was packed off for a summer of indentured servitude in England, where I wandered, on my au-pairing days off, penniless and homesick, burning through my pay with English Ovals and shoplifting willy-nilly in the stores of Oxford Street. I was busted by Top Shop store security with a purse bulging with unpaid-for accessories and was sent back to the States, where my parents greeted me with catalogs for prep schools. They would deal with me once and for all by shipping me off to the only boarding school that would take me, three weeks before the start of the semester. They could no longer handle me, they explained, and they hoped that safely ensconced in the Berkshires, I would be removed from further self-imperilment.

Bud and Banter

I arrived at boarding school a casual, experimental smoker. I left a hardcore addict. In my freshburger anxiety to fit in, I quickly noted that all the cool, funny, interesting people were hanging out in the smoking shed. The school was an ancient summer house whose walls were insulated with old hay. Given the fact that one stray spark could burn it to the ground in under ten minutes, and also given the carelessness and pyromania of teenagers, the faculty had smoking sheds built outside, at a safe distance from the buildings. These sheds were three-sided, wooden lean-to's with benches and institutional-sized coffee cans lined with sand for our butts.

In an attempt to get serious about smoking, I purchased my first carton of cigarettes in town and got to work fitting in with my peers. We were a group of kids in ripped jeans and down parkas, stomping at the frozen earth with our shit-kickers in an attempt to keep blood flowing as we exhaled cumulus clouds of smoke and breath. For a lonely girl, re-jected by her family, there was an implied intimacy and ac-ceptance in smoking that thrilled me: cupped hands around a tiny match or lighting your butt off of someone else's, bumming smokes, letting your friend take a drag without asking. This was the familiarity of smoking, and at times, it felt like love. It brought girls and boys together in an un-spoken alliance, held together by an addiction not only to nicotine, but to shooting the shit.

In the smoking shed there was nothing to do but yap it up and it was in this arena that I discovered and groomed my gift for gab. I learned to flip shit, argue inane points, tell jokes, keep secrets, curse in foreign tongues, write skits, and crib notes from people who were quicker and funnier than I. In the adolescent conversational marketplace, tobacco was our currency. Bumming cigarettes, rolling cigarettes, sharing cigarettes, passing them around, hoarding them until our next trip into town—this was our trade—we negotiated the boundaries of adulthood in a puff of smoke.

If cigarettes were the coin of the realm, then a joint was the jackpot. He Who Held, Ruled. Ganja was subversive, rebellious, smoked on the sly, always with a cigarette burning alongside to cover the smell. Getting stoned took the usual smoking shed banter to new, dizzying heights. Our tangents grew wild and tangled, ideas sprouted, pranks were hatched.

While all the straight kids were up in their dorm rooms keeping up their grade point average, the burners were figuring out ways to beat the system. We communicated in code—a muttered word, a flick of the gaze telegraphed our message: *Let's go blow out.* Under the pretext of "going out for a smoke," we grabbed our parkas, stepped into our Sorrels, and headed out to the shed—or, more often, to the woods beyond the shed. There we would laugh and smoke and brew our dreams. We built secret forts, bugged the faculty room, raided the kitchen, and read things that weren't on the syllabus. After four years I left high school highly educated, deeply addicted to nicotine, and with a visceral understanding that potheads were my people.

Stoned and Deliver

For all this, it may surprise you to learn that I wasn't yet a fullblown pothead. Yes, I loved it and smoked it whenever possible, but this was by no means a daily event. Not even a weekly event. It was occasional at best and remained so all through college. I was more of a passionate hobbyist—I never bought any herb and I never smoked alone. Not since my early forays to Eighty-sixth Street to rendezvous with Jesus had I thrown down for weed. I left that up to my college boyfriend, Jack.

New York City is famous for its home delivery of nearly anything imaginable. Food, flowers, hookers, hardware—if you can dial it up, it can be brought to your door. This, naturally, includes Mary Jane. When he was out of dope, Jack, a can-do guy with a hot sales job, would place a phone call to "A.J." and within a couple of hours a delivery guy in a button-down shirt and khaki pants would be on our doorstep, a discreet manila envelope under his arm. This was better juja than I had ever had, and Jack was something of a connoisseur. You could order from different price points or countries of origin; you could get Thai Sticks of fuzzy red bud or pungent green knots from Humboldt.

Jack grew up in Teaneck, New Jersey, and he and his childhood friends (the "Neckboys") called cannabis "Mike Durgan." This enabled them to be on the phone in front of their parents and say things like, "Is Mike there? I'd like to talk to Mike tonight." Durgan is also known among these wordsmiths as Von Durz or Durvatz. The moniker has hung on and spread to Jack's adulthood friends, who even today say things like, "No thanks, I've already touched Mike tonight."

My love affair with Jack ended, but my affair with Mike endured. Though honestly, it was not an obsessive love. Through my twenties, I saw Mike only casually. I loved Mike when he was around, and didn't miss him much when he wasn't. I remember I bought a bag when I was twenty-five and it lasted until I was twenty-six.

The Grass is Greener

I didn't become a regular user until I had kids. It was the stressful, monotonous, repetitive lifestyle of modern stay-at-home motherhood that turned me into a total, munchy-craving, joint-jonesing, Visine-squirtin' reprobate.

I realize that up until now this has been a fun little past-tense, nostalgic musing on teenage drug use. To talk about our adolescent drug habits as adults is about as shameful as talking about the Moon Boots and culottes we wore back in the '70s. *Aw, who didn't smoke a little grass, man?* But most people grow out of it. Rebelling in high school is a cliché. Smoking bud in college is a rite of passage. But a baked mommy just isn't as nice, is it?

As soon as my children were out of my body, I realized that along with the nearly inexpressible joys of motherhood also comes a terrifying feeling that freedom is lost forever. It was that feeling of being trapped in my home, a feeling I hadn't had since I lived with my mother, that gave me that old, familiar craving to rebel and have a secret life, all my own.

Motherhood comes with sociological expectations that I wasn't interested in living up to. I was expected to comport myself like a grown-up, behaving responsibly at all times, with no other desire in life than to nurture my young. It made me angry. The anger swept up on me and I found myself talking to my children in brusque tones, reprimanding them for things they couldn't help, blowing up in selfish snits over dirty rooms and bad behavior. Who was this exacting, impatient, hard-edged woman I had become? I felt a creepy *déjà vu*, I had seen this before, somewhere before. It felt like I was dressed up as someone else, not myself. But who? Then I realized, I was channelling my own *mother*.

Having children suddenly puts your own childhood into perspective. I saw what a grind it must have been for my mother. The whining, the begging for treats, the temper tantrums. It'll drive anyone to distraction. For women who have been raised and educated to achieve great things in the postfeminist world, motherhood is particularly difficult. All the ideas and dreams your parents pump into you suddenly become irrelevant. It's a weird kind of bait and switch.

Unless you are nannied up to the gills or some kind of über-mamma, you are physically pinned like a butterfly to the tray of domestic life, vainly trying to flap your wings and flit off. Every dream or ambition of success in the larger world that you have cultivated gets plowed under so that your field can now grow these tender little green shoots of new, human life. And though you cherish those lives, are bent to the task of nurturing them, what are you supposed to do with everything else that is inside of you? It can make a gal very, very cranky. It can make her yell at her kids, resent them for being so endlessly needy, want to punish them for things they can hardly help. Rather than do any of those damaging, bad-mommy things, it's tempting to just twist up a nurnypurn and get completely wasted.

Mother's Little Helpers: A History

I'm going to go out on a thin, shaky limb here and say something that may cause some readers to call child services: *Marijuana is a great parenting aid.* I know, I know, it's wrong to have illegal substances around children (no matter how wrongly illegal they may be). But let's just put that irksome legality issue aside and look at the substance itself and its efficacy at keeping edgy moms from totally flipping out.

Motherhood has a long, rich history of substance abuse. In the 1940s mothers used paregoric, a cousin to laudanum, to soothe their frazzled nerves as well as their colicky babies. In the '50s and '60s, housewives were popping Librium to keep on an even keel. My own mother had a prescription for Valium in the '70s which no doubt helped her through many a long day at home with her own rug rats.

In the 1980s, while working women got big shoulder pads and margaritas out with the guys, moms got Xanax. The '90s brought Prozac, smoothing the rough edges off edgy mommies. The twenty-first century so far has brought an uptick in Vicodin abuse, and I know of one mother, who, as I write this, is in the hospital detoxing from it. What's next? Hello OxyContin!

Of course, mother's little helpers aren't all gotten by prescription or dealt on street corners. Throughout the history of stuck-at-home-motherhood runs a river of booze, tobacco, coffee, chocolate, and shopaholicism. How many mothers have I seen, wheeling their sobbing, overtired children through a Ross Dress For Less store, browsing career wear they clearly don't need while their hysterical young try to twist themselves out of their strollers?

It hasn't always been this way. While drugs have been a beautiful thread in the weave of many cultures, their uses have been more ceremonial than maintenance. Historically, pharmaceuticals and stay-at-home motherhood rose simultaneously. Coincidence? I wonder if a study has ever been done on drug abuse and the advent of the modern housewife? If I weren't so lazy and distractible, I would research it. I bet I'd find a direct correlation.

Back in the old pre-industrial-revolution days, there were no such things as stay-at-home moms. All moms stayed at home, and home is where the extended family lived. Dad was out plowing the fields and hunting game, Grandma was by the fireplace, knitting little sweaters with her gnarled fingers. Sis was helping you get dinner on, and all of your children were playing out in front of the house without you having to stand on the doorstep mentally noting the license plate numbers of every passing van. There were stresses, of course. Would Indians attack? Would a swarm of locusts eat your crops? But those were external worries. Those moms didn't have one hundred years of psychotherapy telling them they were fucking-up their kids. If kids got fucked-up, then it was the Devil's work and not your fault. Fire, flood, famine surely suck, but are nothing beside the daily fear that your kid's psyche is in your hands, and no matter what you do, she is going to spend a lifetime in therapy because you were a crabby, bitchy, resentful mom.

Why so crabby and stressed? What did that pioneer mom raising her kids in the proverbial village have that we modern moms with all our vaunted modern conveniences lack? Well, for one thing, they had *adult conversation*. They weren't raising kids in a mental/conversational vacuum. They were having quilting bees, shucking corn together, hanging out at barn dances, passing down that rich oral tradition we've heard so much about, but were left out of the loop on. While they told their children stories that explained the universe both within and outside of their beings, at the end of the day we have to read our toddlers *Barney Goes to Work* yet again, in which we endlessly revisit the dentist to learn about proper oral hygiene.

Cooking and cleaning weren't undervalued in the Old World, because without it the family would perish. Nobody gave a damn about freshness or Downy-softness, or anything being tight as a drum. It was all slaughter, skin, salt, and store. Women didn't have to worry about making time in their day for exercise because just putting dinner on the table burned about 5,000 calories. And if they did happen to get a little zaftig? It was all well-hidden under voluminous skirts. Husbands would relish the lifting of those skirts, the revealing of the dimpled, fleshy keister. Every wife was a trophy.

Pioneer women didn't worry about their unrealized career potential, because there weren't any careers for women. Not that that in and of itself didn't suck, but at least they didn't have to feel like losers in stretch pants a single day of their lives.

Any given day in the life of a modern mother is a pastiche of chores, routines, and time-killing activities that you perform until you can finally put your children to bed. You are not a brave pioneer protecting your young from starvation and rabid prairie dogs; you are the person who knows how to poke the straw into the juice box. You are the person who cuts the crusts off of sandwiches. You are the person who follows your toddler around the house, through sandboxes, down the street, picking up whatever debris she tosses aside in the course of her own tiny life adventure. You are your child's handmaiden, and though your work is defended by feminists as heroic, noble, essential—secretly, in your heart, you undervalue it like everyone else because you know it's unskilled labor. All it takes is a set of milky jugs and a relentless, instinctual urge to see your child make it through another day alive. You bring all your education, experience and know-how to the task of butt-wiping, and use your hard-won negotiation skills to say "no, no, no" until the word becomes a strange mantra lacking all meaning for either of you.

The hardest part of motherhood, for me, is constantly making decisions about issues I am not trained to assess or deal with, such as: Can she have another cookie if she's already had three? *I don't know.* Should I let her have bubbles in the tub, even though it gives her an itchy vagina?

Again, I don't know. Should she give the toy back, even though she said she had it first? *God fucking dammit! I don't know! I don't know, and frankly I don't care!* This is the moment when you park your kid in front of Blues Clues, sneak your pipe from its hiding place, and slip out to the backyard for a quick puff.

Call it "me time"—a backyard buzz is a mini spa vacation for the brain. Two hits and suddenly a deep calm comes over you. The tension that moments ago made you feel as though your skin were stuffed with Brillo pads eases, and the world around you stops clattering and falls into a soothing hum.

That pile of dirty breakfast dishes festering in your sink? It becomes a creative challenge rather than a chore. Cooking dinner is an opportunity for nutritional art-making set to the dulcet tones of Noah Adams. Doing the laundry is a teachable moment, as you let your toddler pour the detergent and pull out the dial on the machine. And your child? In the post-buzz glow, your whiny task-mistress becomes a sweet cherub wrapped in a halo of light. You clasp her to your saggy breast (hoping she won't wonder why you smell like smoke) and vow to make the most of every day with her. Because living with a child is living in a state of grace. All the potential of the universe is stored within her precious soul, and raising her may be the single greatest creative act of your life.

Dazed and Confused

Previous to motherhood, I had been a svelte, rising actress-about-town. I had appeared on a hit sitcom and in a noted independent film. I had, as they say out here in Hollywood, "heat." But I made the terrible career move of getting knocked up. Then I made the even worse career move of eating my way through my pregnancy. I gained an absurd amount of weight, which resulted in a healthy, robust ten-and-a-half-pound infant and in me being a healthy, robust, two-hundred-pound postpartum person.

Nevertheless, I still thought I could make it work. In those first months after Franny was born I persisted in going on auditions. I would squeeze myself into tight outfits and drive out to casting calls, my old headshot staring up at me from the passenger seat, mocking me. *"Who do you think you are?"* that younger, thinner Erika seemed to say. *"They're not going to hire you to play a lawyer. You can't even negotiate terms with a babysitter, you fat cow."* I prayed I would be able to get through my readings before I started leaking milk through my I-am-not-a-professional-person-but-I-am-attempting-to-play-one-on-TV silk audition blouse.

Finally there was one terrible day when my daughter was four months old and I found myself trying to make it to an audition in the Valley. My sitter had shown up late, and I tried taking shortcuts but just ended up driving in traffic-riddled circles, hitting one dead end after another. My breasts were engorged and prickly, I was bathed in sweat, and sobbing, just sobbing, because I knew I was not going to be a professional anything for a long, long time, if ever, and that the dream of stardom I had burnished since girlhood was over. In fact, girlhood itself was over, and that in and of itself bode ill for my future stardom. Two months later my agent, the agent who had so passionately sought me out, who had lunched me into a lather a year earlier and filled me with promises of fame, sent me a form letter on agency letterhead terminating our contract. It arrived the day before my first Mother's Day. I decided over brunch that Sunday that I was done with actressing for good.

I decided I would take my creative life by the horns. Can't leave the house? Fine. I'll stay home and create. I put my one-year-old in daycare-lite, giving myself three hours a day to work on an idea I had for a one-woman show.

Over the course of pregnancy, childbirth, and baby-rearing, I had come to see that I was just a pawn in a Darwinian *fait accompli*. Everything I had done in my life was just my hormones leading me into this corral. I had been sucked into motherhood like the *Enterprise* in a Klingon tractor beam. Though I fancied myself a confident Captain Kirk, sitting jauntily at the bridge of my life, I was, in fact, Scotty, caught in the bowels of the ship, yelling, "We just don't have enough power, Cap'n!" The overwhelming, hypnotic, almost terrifying love I felt for my young merely freaked me out even more. Not only was I caught in a life of mind-numbing, mundane repetition, but were that to be taken away for any reason, I would have to kill myself, or walk the earth a wasted shell of a woman. I thought that would make a fun show, so I sat down to write it.

Fear Pressure

Now, at this point you may think, how much worse can this woman's addiction get? But though my herb use increased with the arrival of children, I still only used it in case of emergency. My little spa sessions out by the compost pile happened only when I had exhausted all my other resources: after I had reached out to girlfriends on the phone, eaten all the mint Milanos, and used nap time to rev up the vibrator.

No, I didn't become a full-on, wakin' and bakin', gargling-before-school-pickup, hit-towel-usin' mom until I decided to write. The thing that pushed me over the edge into daily drug abuse was fear.

I am the latest in a long line of writers in my family. My parents, grandparents, uncle, cousins, sister—all writers. In my family, writing is a genetic illness. Like any inherited trait, I showed signs of it as a child. I kept journals, wrote poems, edited pretend newspapers, penned endless skits, authored a number of song lyrics, and wrote book reports that my teachers scribbled stars, checks, plusses, and smiley faces on. It was assumed by all that I would go into the family business.

Unlike the rest of the world, I did not view the writing life as romantic. I watched my father ply his trade doggedly, tethered to his typewriter, churning out film reviews, opinion pieces, and one thick, sparsely illustrated book after another. Deadlines spiked our family life with tension, our fortunes rose and fell with the tides of the periodical marketplace, and my father's workaholism brewed a rancid tea of resentment in our home. While most families spent weekends together, picnicking or flying kites in the park, my family was held in thrall to my father's important work. My mother, also a writer, managed to produce two novels and a smattering of magazine pieces in the course of raising me and my sister (a feat I am now in awe of), but her smaller career was meted out on the sidelines of family life. As far as I was concerned, writing was not an art or a noble calling or a heroic act of creativity; writing was the thing that distracted my parents from me.

So I never dreamed of being a pencil pusher. Anyone who ever spent a single day with a writer could see that it completely lacked glamour. No, my dream (original only in the context of my family) was to be a star of stage and screen. Not only did it seem more rewarding, but stating it repeatedly was a way of letting my parents know that I was going to break free of the family curse and be my own self.

But on that terrible first Mother's Day, after my agents had dumped me, the family curse finally caught up with me. I realized that getting out of the house was not really an option for me, and that whatever creativity I pursued would have to be done at the dining room table.

After a lifetime of saying I wasn't going to be a writer, I had convinced myself I wasn't a writer. I sat for days at my computer, looking at the blinking cursor, terrified of writing something that would suck. Then, after several days of this horrifying creative constipation, I heard a whisper in my ear: *If you smoke it, it will come.* For the first time in my life I blew out to work, and it kicked down the door of my creative inhibitions and *Wild Amerika* came pouring out. I smoked every day for a month as I gushed this show onto the page. I romped in the fields of my imagination, saying "YES!" to everything, and feeling for the first time in my life that I was doing what I was meant to do. It was the most ecstatic, liberating experience of my life and it transformed me not only into a full-time writer, but into a full-time stoner.

Slacker Mom

I'd like to take a moment to dispel a cliché about stoners that has dogged us for decades. There is an image of the pothead as a slacking, unmotivated, fuzzy-headed loser. While admittedly there are those who wake, bake, and then spend their days playing Nintendo and sucking cheese out of a can, in my experience they have been the exception and not the rule. The stoners I have known have been creative, motivated, responsible, and upstanding citizens in every respect other than the fact that they are breaking the law by smoking pot.

I myself didn't smoke hay to avoid work, but smoked so I could work more. In my ten years as a hard-core user I maintained some pretty high standards. In addition to raising two girls (who so far are turning out to be relatively undamaged), I have written most of this book, directed two musicals at my daughters' grade school, started a student newspaper, planted several gardens, learned how to knit, cooked innumerable meals, kept a (reasonably) clean house, run a marathon, ghost-written a yoga book, pumped my own gas, made it to a lifetime membership at Weight Watchers, and in general have been a contributing member of society. I was a very high functioning addict.

Most days saw me wasted. I would spark up as soon as my kids were off to school or daycare. My buzz and my writing day would end around two, at which point I would vainly try to refresh myself with a shower and some vigorous tooth-brushing. I would arrive daily to pick my kids up from school and other moms would say, "Are you okay? You look tired."

"Oh, I'm not sleeping well," would be my reply, too embarrassed to admit I had been home smoking rope like a tenth-grader on spring break.

Busted

As with all substance abuse, my high got harder to achieve. I'd smoke and experience five minutes of euphoria followed by five hours of exhaustion and regret. I felt I was a failure at living through the day. I couldn't hack it in the world everyone else lived in. Whatever motivation I initially got from my buzz would quickly dissipate and I'd find myself acting like a stooge, wandering around the house trying to remember what it was I meant to do in the first place.

"I smell smoke," my perceptive children would occasionally say when I leaned in for a kiss, their eyes question marks. I was cornered. They knew the evils of cigarette smoking, so I couldn't lie and tell them I had been huffing butts. But how to explain what mommy was really up to?

"Oh, I was burning some sage," I'd lamely offer, hoping that I wouldn't also burn in hell for lying to my babes. I'd hustle away, hoping to avoid any follow-up questions. But they were growing up and getting wise to mommy's jive.

Then, finally, came the day of reckoning. In a wasted stupor I left my head can out. It was a small canister with a "Dazed and Confused" sticker on it. Movie swag. In it I kept my pipe, my papers, my lighter, my mini Play-Doh tub of weed. The girls found it and brought it to me, full of questions.

"What's this, Mommy?" I was busted. I panicked, fumbled. I had nothing to offer but the truth. "Okay, kids, sometimes I smoke something that helps me relax. It's not dangerous, but it is illegal."

"What's illegal, Mommy?" asked my six-year-old.

"Against the law, honey." God, this was weird. Was I committing another crime by talking about this? Should I just lie? "Sometimes grown-ups make their own decisions about what rules they are going to follow. It's important not to break rules that will hurt other people. Stealing is always wrong. Hurting people is always wrong." Was I hurting my children by telling them this? There weren't any chapters in any of the parenting books I had ever read on this subject. I was adrift in uncharted parenting waters here. "But I don't feel that this thing I sometimes smoke is wrong or bad. Someday hopefully everyone will agree that it's not that harmful and it won't be illegal anymore. But for now, I have to keep it a secret. Do you understand?" They nodded and said they understood, but I was more confused than ever.

It took me another four months before I came up with the courage to quit, and that was only two months ago. But that was the beginning of the end. I never wanted to be in a position of justifying to my kids why it was okay to break the law, no matter how wrongheaded I felt that law was. Also, I realized that I needed to try life straight for a while, if only to see what it was like.

It takes a while to hit bottom, then a little longer to realize that that thing you're scraping against *is the bottom*. Especially with the green goddess. Pot addiction is a walk in the park compared to other addictions. You don't end up broke, with kidney failure, or blacked out on the bathroom floor with a needle hanging out of your arm. Very few potheads end up turning tricks or knocking off convenience stores to get their next high. If we're in a convenience store, its usually to buy a Slurpee and a bag of chips late at night.

But I felt the wear and tear of my addiction. I was tired of being so, so, SO tired at the end of the day. I was sick of coming down with swollen glands and a head cold every six weeks because I had taxed my immune system with smoke. I knew that I was forgetting things, but even worse, that I was missing things. I was using weed to check out, to run away from the things I didn't want to confront: fear and anger. I wanted to be with my family firsthand. I wanted to wake up in the morning without feeling charred. I wanted to remember the little things, like where I had read something and what it was. Or who it was I had told something to. Details got lost in the churning chum bucket that was my brain on drugs.

I wanted to stop constantly worrying about throat, mouth, and lung cancer. I was convinced that the smoke, combined with all the particulate matter I breathe in as a resident of Los Angeles, was going to kill me. I wanted to write this essay, but I had to be straight to do it. This way, when the D.E.A. is tipped off to my bad behavior, they won't find anything when they come to search my house. See, this is all *past* tense.

A New Leaf

All of these things were motivating me toward quitting, but none of it really did the trick. Finally, the thing that made me quit was something so superficial I am almost ashamed to admit it. I wanted to clear up my skin.

Over the course of years, my skin, which had always been zit-free and radiant, became distressingly pizza-like. It started with a few blemishes, and bloomed into full-on acne. My cheeks were covered with deep, cyst-like lumps that wouldn't squeeze and resolve, but hung around for weeks, sometimes months. I saw facialists and tried expensive creams and lotions, astringents and peels, but nothing worked. For a while I blamed it on the crappy L.A. air, but then one day, while researching it on the Internet, I learned that skin problems are almost always caused by toxins in the liver. Now, other than sugar, what toxins was I ingesting regularly? Ah. I stopped smoking dope and my skin cleared up.

I am aware that some of my readers may not be dope smokers. I have lived my life in New York and Los Angeles, and I know that out in the vast middle of the country, splim smoking is done mostly by bored teenagers, not bored housewives. But where I live, the mohasky is everywhere. Moms, dads, yoga teachers, editors, *nearly everyone I know in Los Angeles smokes pot.* It's one of the reasons I have found it so hard to quit. The peer pressure is considerable. Just when I think I might like to stop, someone passes me a smoking joy stick.

When I first quit, I became frozen. For three weeks I could neither shit nor write. I would alternate between my desk and my bathroom, sitting quietly and patiently, waiting for inspiration to release me, but it didn't come. Sometimes I could pinch off a mingy little paragraph or two, but there was no real movement. I longed for a purgative puff.

Quitting was bad for me creatively. I used to mow the grass with friends and yap for hours, ending up with three new ideas for projects. Now I sat at my desk waiting for inspiration, this book deadline looming, feeling like I had chosen the worst possible time to go straight. Why would I mess with my lucky combination? I saw my great creative fear manifesting: I was writing things that sucked.

Sucking it Up

In desperation, I turned to meditation, hoping I might be able to reach the same psychic place I once occupied stoned. I went to a local "woo-woo" bookstore. The Bodhi Tree is a venerable West Hollywood institution, a haven for the zillions of mystics, faith healers, and alternative lifestylers that gravitate to Los Angeles. The store is a warren of tightly packed bookcases, scented with incense, tinkling with wind chimes, and awash in the soothing tones of Enya.

I found a clerk in dreadlocks and Birkenstocks who showed me where the meditation CDs were kept, next to the section on addiction and recovery. "What are you looking for specifically?" he asked.

"Well, I'm not sure. Something that can help with creativity . . . I just gave up an addiction and I'm having a little trouble focusing on my work."

"What was your addiction?" he pressed, looking at me with big, trustworthy brown eyes.

"Um . . . cannabis."

"Why are you quitting that? It's not like its heroin or crack. My advice is go back to smoking pot."

This was the reaction of a lot of people I know. Nobody seemed to think a person could smoke too much reefer. Pot is so common and beloved in my community, I felt like a traitor for giving it up. On the day I quit I gave my stash to my friend Matt, who took it reluctantly. "You're sure you want to do this?"

"Yeah, I have to."

"Okay, but I'll always have some if you want it."

"I know."

"Because you know you love the blow out."

"Yes, Matt, I do. But I'm quitting anyway."

"Okay, it's your life."

I didn't miss Miss Jane all the time, but sometimes I felt overcome with longing. I wanted to inhale and exhale my dreams. I wanted to feel the liftoff that comes with the first couple of hits. That feeling where your toes come off the ground, and suddenly you are flying over your life, seeing it from a new perspective—a crazy-quilt of possibility. Ideas rush in, inspiration strikes. But even more than that, I missed the taste of smoke in my mouth.

Giving up the chronic isn't as hard as giving up cigarettes was. It's not physically addicting. I wasn't twitchy, or sick, or shaking. Yes, I jonesed, but it was more from missing the habit psychologically. I would get ready to go work in my garden and wish I could smoke a joint and forget myself in the project. Everywhere I went, there I was.

It's hard to give up something you believe in. I believe in Durgan. I believe it should be made legal because, sprinkled in moderation, it is one of the spices of life. It can season an ordinary day with dreams and deep thought. Passed around between friends, it is like a tiny hearth, around which we gather to laugh and talk and be as dorky as we dare. I reject the notion that marijuana is a gateway to stronger drugs. Though it's true I've tried stronger drugs, none of them stuck. Sure, crackheads probably smoked pot first, but show me a crackhead who isn't also smoking a pack of cigarettes a day. If you're gonna be a junkie, then you'll be one whether or not you smoke astro turf.

Brave New Girl

I don't know what I'll do when my kids get old enough to smoke. It won't terrify me like it does other parents. I'd much rather they smoke a mezzarola with their underage friends than drink. By then they will probably have read this essay, and, hopefully, knowing their mom was a cheeb head, will reject it as totally uncool. If I do find a stash while cleaning their rooms (unlikely, as I rarely clean their rooms), then I'm more likely to bite the bud than bite their heads off.

I actually worry about my kids growing up in a world with no reasonable smoking outlets. While I certainly don't want them to be addicted to cigarettes and pot as I was, I wonder how and where they'll hang out. Will they just be coldly instant-messaging their friends from a safe distance? Will they gather in smoke-free shopping malls or huddle around the glow of a PDA, watching videos, never experiencing the friction, intimacy, and conversation that comes from lighting a match and sharing a smoke? What will their taboo behavior be? How will they press against the boundaries of childhood?

As a parent I want to take a responsible position against smoking, because I understand it is bad for the body, but in my heart, I believe it is good for the mind. Up to a point, of course. Living without moral absolutes can be a lot of work. One must constantly be reviewing the latest evidence.

I will always be a burner, even when I am not smoking. Not smoking makes me feel like an amputee with a phantom limb. What's missing is that smoldering stick between my lips, that smokestack that vents the fire that has burned inside me since I was born. I am enjoying the clearheadedness and the increased lung capacity of my current non-smoking state. I hope this clean living will lead to a longer, healthier, more productive life, but sometimes I wonder—is that really the life I was meant to live?

I'm gonna go build a fire and think about it some more.

Sisters

Franny and Georgia are out in the backyard playing together. They are each dressed as a fantasy version of themselves: Franny is in a long, demure prairie dress with contrasting apron, and Georgia is teetering in high heels, miniskirt, and a red tube top. It's Laura Ingalls Wilder meets Iris from *Taxi Driver*. Little Whorehouse on the Prairie.

The girls have been fighting all morning. Competing for the shake at the bottom of the Lucky Charms box, the TV clicker, my attention. I am on a deadline and in a parenting gaffe I have neglected to arrange Saturday play dates for them. Doug is, as usual, occupied with various tweak-based activities in the garage, and left to their own devices, my outside-stimulus-addicted kids have been at each other's throats. "I *hate* Franny!!" seven-year-old Georgia screamed at me an hour ago, her face bunched into angry tears. Franny, eyes set and lip quivering with perceived injustice and ten-year-old 'tween rage, stalked off into her room, slamming the door behind her. I have tried mediation in the past, but nowadays I just let them deal with it themselves. This relationship doesn't need work, this is just how it works. They fight, squabble, compare, compete, bicker, sulk, and finally, when bored of all that, they play. And when they play, they are divine.

I am watching them from my office, which has a view of the backyard. Franny has a small wicker basket slung over her arm in which she has been gathering nasturtium blossoms. The blossoms will likely either end up in a small, surprise vase on my bedside table, or they will adorn the many fairy houses Franny has hidden around our garden. Franny is in her Thoreau mode, contemplating nature and lost in her own deep thoughts. Meanwhile, Georgia is negotiating the tire swing in her high heels. She launches herself off the top of the Playskool toddler slide (now kept solely as a swing launch) and narrowly misses arcing into the corner of the playhouse. Unfazed by yet another near-skull-puncture, Georgia calls out to her sister, "Do you want to play pretend?"

"Okay, " amenable Fran replies.

From my desk I can hear their voices ramp with excitement. Franny's voice, usually set low and dulcet, picks up pace with ideas for the game. "Let's pretend its olden times, and we live in a village, and it's war, and . . ."

Georgia's voice, high and clear like a record cranked a notch too fast, chimes in, "Yeah, and let's pretend we're sisters!"

"Yeah!" Franny agrees. "I'm the older sister."

"Okay, I'm the little sister, but we're both teenagers!"

This is one of their favorite games, and it always makes me laugh. *Pretending* you are sisters is completely different from *being* sisters. Most of the imaginary games the girls play, whether together or with friends, center around a pair of sisters. Through the archetype of sisterhood the girls can express their deepest fealty. For as everyone knows, the bond between sisters is as deep as any that exists. They cling to each other in thick and thin, risking their lives for each other. The dialogue in these games features lines like, *Yes, Sister! I am coming, Sister!* and *Oh Sister, be careful!!"* Sisters are fiercely united and able to endure any kind of hardship, because they have each other.

Or so I've heard. I don't have many memories of my own little sister when we were young, even though Jessica and I lived at home together for a total of nine years. But the nearly four-year age difference between us kept our interests separate most of the time. I mainly remember her being a pain in the ass: horning in on me and my friends, taking up too much room in the backseat of the car, tattling on me at the drop of a hat. We kept constant vigil over our separate boundaries, hoarding our stuff and our friends. She was a bratty little sister and I was just mean. I still have a club diary Jilly and I had. One page has this: Jilly = (drawing of beautiful rose), Erika = (drawing of lovely daisy), Jessie = (drawing of stinky, putrid garbage can).

The girls continue their separate activities as they develop the details of their game. This is the best part of pretend—making up the back story. "My name is Clara and I'm seventeen," Franny says as she continues picking flowers. Her sister fantasy is always very nineteenth century, heavily influenced by Frances Hodgson Burnett and frequently features orphans. She continues picking flowers, but the activity has become a sense-memory exercise for her. Her body language changes from dogged pursuit of the most saturated blooms to a more lilting, theatrical step as she finds her character.

Georgia does lazy spirals on the tire swing, her head

back, the fine ends of her long hair feathering in the breeze as she contemplates her own character. "Okay, my name is Miranda, and I have long, long, silky hair." (Silky hair is Georgia's great desire, her *raison d'être*. One time, on a boring car ride, I asked her, Franny, and Franny's friend Olivia if they had three wishes, what they would wish for. The big girls answered responsibly and predictably: *World peace, the end of diseases . . . and three more wishes.* Georgia silently considered, then answered, *World peace, the end of diseases . . . and silky hair.*)

Orphaned by a bomb, the two sisters have fled the city. They must make their way through the bombed-out city to the train station, where they will escape. Slowly their bodies are drawn into the fantasy. Georgia unthreads her legs from the tire and kicks off her pumps, picking up a length of PVC pipe to use as a sword. Franny dumps the already wilting nasturtiums out of her basket onto the picnic table and runs into the house to requisition some supplies. Since she was a toddler, Franny has always enjoyed packing for her adventures. All her life I have found bags and boxes and purses and bandanas filled with necessaries: a *Betty and Veronica Digest,* a roll of pennies, a jump rope, a small, ceramic cat—the totems that protect Fran in her imaginary world.

I don't remember playing many games with my sister. Among my very few isolated memories of our childhood together, two stand out vivdly. For a long time Jesssie and I had a morning ritual in which we would "clap out" dresses for each other. We stood before our bedroom closet looking at the long row of beautiful dresses our mother had bought for us at Bloomingdale's and Bonwit Teller's. We were well turned-out girls and had matching Marimekko and Gunne Sax sister dresses that in family photographs make us look like harmonious twins, and not the fractious, squabbling siblings we actually were.

The rule of our game was we couldn't speak, but only "clap out" the dresses, smacking them wordlessly yet approvingly. We always gave each other a couple of choices. My sister had a doggie dress that we both agreed was the best dress ever. It had a bodice, a tiered skirt, and a pattern of many breeds of dog heads rendered in near-photographic detail. I clapped that one out for her a lot, because I knew she always wanted to wear it. That felt to me like love.

The other memory is also inside the closet. I am ten and my sister is six and a half, and we are in the closet, buried deep in the back row of winter dresses. We are crouched on a pile of dusty Tretorns and scuffed Mary Janes, our beautiful clothes muffling the sound of our parents' angry voices woofing at each other through the walls. I am holding her close and telling her over and over, *Don't worry, Jessie, it's just a fight—they won't get divorced.*

Our parents divorced a couple of years later, dividing up everything they owned: records, books, friends—us. Jessie went out West with Mom (and Mom's boyfriend, Frank, Jilly's dad), and I went to boarding school, spending most of my vacation time with my father in New York. I never officially lived with my sister again.

I did pay a few long visits, however, beginning the summer after my freshman year. I went to Santa Fe and stayed with my mom, sister, and Frank. I remember looking at my sister's new, freshly painted bedroom and realizing that I no longer had context within this part of the family. I spent the summer scooping ice cream at the Swensen's parlor on Water Street, fighting with Mom, and trying to spend as much time away from the house as humanly possible. I don't remember what my sister was doing that summer.

Probably just trying to make some new friends in her new town.

One afternoon my mother took me and my sister to an Olde Tyme photography studio off the main square to have a sepia-toned portrait taken for our grandmother's birthday. We dressed up as western fantasy versions of ourselves. My sister picked out an Annie Oakley getup: plaid skirt, vest, cowboy cuffs, and a six-shooter at her hip. I chose the sluttiest dress I could find: a satin, off-the-shoulder number with velvet ruffs and a wide, velvet choker.

When my grandmother died a few years ago, I inherited the photograph, and it now hangs in my hallway, where the girls and I frequently stop to marvel at it. I am seated with one hand on a fan in my lap, the other on my hip. Under the deep brim of a feathered hat, my eyes smolder with surliness, my jaw set with nascent teen defiance, my small, newly minted breasts thrust forward with the confidence of someone who has been told she is jail bait. Beside me, my nine-year-old sister stands, holding a rifle, her face nearly a blank. We are clearly strangers to each other. This is the only photograph I know of that was taken of us together during our entire adolescence.

Clara and Miranda, the pretend sisters, have made it to the train station and board a train (picnic benches lined up in rows) that is to take them away to a Narnia-like land where they will be given magic powers. But there is a ghost on the train, haunting and threatening them. Armed only with hose attachments, which in their game will spray a blinding fog, they must escape the ghost and get to the safety of the magic land.

"Sister, hold my hand! We must flee this evil!" Franny cries out, protectively grabbing Georgia's hand like she will never let go.

* * *

It wasn't until Jessica and I were both in college that we found our way back to each other. In the liberal and neutral territory of off-campus housing, we discovered on periodic visits that we actually rather liked each other. Though we felt more like distant cousins than sisters—people who shared blood and a few isolated childhood memories, but had no real context together. But my now-grown sister had lost her bratty ways and revealed herself to me as someone I enjoyed. She was wickedly funny, had great taste in music, knew how to whip up a nice lunch, and had terrific friends. Many of those friends, upon meeting me, would say, *Wow, you must be Jessica's sister!* Like twins separated at birth, we had grown up to be strangely, latently identical. We were both vivid, bantering, shit-flipping girls. We laughed the same way at the same things, gestured alike, and when we answered each other's phones, callers could not tell us apart. We had always thought we were nothing alike. Our differences had always been pointed out to us, but never our similarities. It came as a huge surprise to us both.

"Mooooooommmy! Franny hit me!!" Georgia stands in the doorway, scowling. Franny pulls up behind her, ready with her defense, "I did not. It was an accident."

"It was *not,* Mom. She hit me hard on the forehead." I can tell by her tone of voice that Georgia is not in the least hurt.

"All I did was this." Franny presses her palm against Georgia's forehead, replaying the offense.

"Ooh—actually, that feels kinda good," Georgia says, giggling. "Do it again." Franny does and they both crack up and turn back out to the yard, back to their game. I resume my position at the computer, another conflict successfully negotiated not by me.

When I learned I was pregnant with a second girl, I became gripped by anxiety. Though I was happy having one daughter, having two would put me in danger of replicating my original family. I wanted to create a completely new family. I wanted to break the all-girl precedent set by my parents. I wanted to try my hand at raising a boy, perhaps even succeeding where so many other mothers had clearly failed, by raising one into capable, sensitive, exemplary manhood. But two blond, city-bred girls? No, that was just too close to home.

"I think you were meant to have girls," Ali tells me. "The world needs more strong women and you're just the gal to make some." Ali is a bonus sister I picked up in high school. We had been assigned to each other as roommates our freshman year, and I was as mean to her as I had been to my sister back when we were little. A spoiled only child, Ali got "Care packages" from her mother in California which bulged with goodies a dorm-starved girl dreams of late at night. She had cans of squeeze cheese, boxes of Triscuits, bags of Milanos, mix-up lemonade. I imagined this faraway mother lovingly packing up snacks for Ali while my own mother packed my stuff into boxes to put into storage. I hated Ali and set myself to making her life a living hell, teasing her, short-sheeting her bed, raiding her supplies whenever possible.

Over the next couple of years Ali and I found ourselves gradually coming to like each other in spite of our bad beginning and our many differences. In our junior year, out of a perverse sense of . . . "whatever" . . . we signed up to be roomies again. We were discovering the uncommon pleasures of a friendship founded on initial mutual dislike. It was that very spring, at an Arts Weekend for parents, that my father and her mother met and fell in love.

Having already lost my best friend (and former play "sister") Jilly when my mother shacked up with her dad, Frank, I was not psyched when my alpha-dad laid eyes on the beautiful, elegant, statuesque Carol, as she wafted up the school steps in a silk pantsuit. My dad and I were sitting on the porch, smoking cigarettes, and as Carol floated past in a cloud of Anäis, he turned to me and with a raised eyebrow asked, "Who dat?"

I could see it coming. Ali and I resigned ourselves to the inevitable and were able to make the best of what turned out to be, for a while, a very bad situation.

Carol had many fine qualities (generosity, humor, intelligence, poise) but her one fatal flaw was her near-paranoid insecurity. She was afraid of me, and even more threatened by my sister. She dedicated herself to engineering a rift between Jessica and my father that to this day scars them both. While Jess had never been much of a presence in my father's life since the divorce, when Carol married into the family, Jessica quickly became *persona non grata*. Caught up in my own familial turmoil, and not knowing my sister well enough to defend her effectively, I sat back and mutely watched her get the shaft.

When I was twenty-five, Jessica came out to Los Angeles, where Dad and Carol were living and where I had recently moved. One night, after a typically tense family dinner, Jess and I found ourselves in my parked car in front of our father's house, smoking a bowl. We started talking about ourselves, telling each other the story of our lives. The conversation unspooled for nearly four hours, as we burned through a pack of cigarettes and a few more pipeloads of pot. We discovered how much we had in common, beyond just mannerisms and a mutual love of salty talk. We discovered that despite our separate childhoods, we had grown up to be very much the same on the inside, too. All these years we had been walking around with the same feelings and symptoms—the same problems in our relationships with men, the same memory loss from our childhood, the same loneliness and sense of guilt and failure. It was like falling in love, discovering each other and how much we had in common. We laughed and sobbed and said, *I know! Me, too!*" over and over again. Though I had been in love before, never had I felt so completed by another person as I did that night by my own sister.

Franny and Georgia are looking through a rack of Western costumes. We are weekending in Solvang, and have come upon an Olde Tyme photography studio. We have decided it would be a gas to hang a similar photo of them next to the one of me and Auntie Jessie. Georgia comes upon a royal blue velvet dress with a lace collar, and finding it suitably twirly, she puts the backless costume on like a hospital gown over her jeans and t-shirt. Franny finds a demure lavender dress in *peau de soie*. Though my girls are not quite as old as my sister and I were when our brooding portrait was taken in Santa Fe, nevertheless there are similarities. Franny looks very much like me. She is broad-shouldered and intense, womanhood beginning to dawn in her gray eyes. Georgia looks uncannily like Jessica. She has the same build, the same clear blue eyes and sassy mouth. In fact, she looks more like my niece than my daughter. But the big difference between this set of sisters and the pair from thirty years ago is they are clearly enjoying each other.

"Franny, Franny . . ." Georgia asks, trying on a hat, "Do you like this one?"

"Oh Georgia, you look sooo cute!" Franny enthuses. "Here, let me fix your hair." These girls know each other better than anyone else in the world. They are sisters who are friends, and friends who are sisters. The photographer poses them in front of the antique camera. Franny sits in a chair, her hands folded over a small book of sonnets in her lap. Georgia stands beside her, holding not a rifle, but a parasol. The camera flashes and after a short wait we are handed a sepia-toned photograph of two smiling girls.

Ali was right—I was meant to have girls. I was meant to see this relationship succeed, and take part in tending it. My girls are making up for all the time my sister and I lost, and it fills me with a deep hum of joy.

The summer after Doug and I were married, Carol died suddenly and quickly of cancer. In the way of tragic illness, it snapped our family out of its petty, myopic drama and made us rise to our best selves. I discovered I could let go of my anger and be a rock for other people. Ali, suddenly a motherless child, let go of her childish ways and bloomed into one of the most solid people I have known. Ali and I decided that though the legal tie that held us to each other as sisters had passed, we were bonded for life. Looking back on the near-thirty years we have known each other, I realize now Ali came into my life at nearly the exact moment my blood sister was removed from it. Pretend sisters we may be, but the loyalty we feel toward each other animates us and feels as real as anything.

Jessica has children of her own now, too, a boy and a girl, and we are once again living half a continent apart. We have spent many long-distance hours discussing our lives, present, past, and future. It is difficult to communicate what she means to me, so profound is her role in my life and psyche. She holds the combination to my soul. Through that divine soup of genetics, experience, and disposition, we have come to be each other's closest allies. Only we really understand how we ended up being the way we are, and that knowledge keeps us safe somehow. We protect each other when the ghost on the train is chasing us. Of course, we still push each other's buttons, and are capable of thoroughly pissing each other off, but the relationship doesn't need work, it's just how it works.

The pretend sisters have come upon some fresh danger in their game. "Quickly, Sister!" Georgia shouts. "We must hide!" They cower behind a lawn chair, their arms flung around each other, flushed and panting. "Don't worry, Sister," Franny assures Georgia. "We'll be all right."

That, I happen to know, is a fact.